Drawn from a Vietnam photograph by author's son, Joseph Frederic

1

PRELUDE

This book has been rolling around in my brain for most of 50 years. During that time, I have told parts of my story to as many as would take the time to listen. Most of those have been friends and family or acquaintances that have interest in the Vietnam War.

Thank you ALL for hearing. Some of you recall when the wounds were fresh. Words of a young man still speaking in the language of war. You know who you are. All of you were kind to me, those who sat with me at points along this transition.

For help with this book,

Thank you first to my wife Janet, for seeing the positive in me and not giving up.

Thank you to my sister Kathy for your help and enlisting the aid of your son, Warrant Officer Todd Bobeda, in editing and encouraging.

Thank you to all my children for their love and support.

Thank you to my old friend Tim Wheeler, who has heard parts of my story so many times that he could write them himself.

Thanks to my four brothers, Kit, Kelly, Kevin, and Jim for the strength we gather from each other.

Thanks to the doctors, nurses, clinicians and mental health professionals that have had a hand in this journey towards healing.

Last, Thank you God for such an amazing experience on this planet!

DISCLAIMER

Diaper Dan is a real story about me and the people and events that came along during my time. The only research that has been done is to search my own memory. These are the events as I remember them. Some of the names have been changed or substituted for lack of memory. If you see yourself in any of these pages... Congratulations on being alive and I wish you well.

DIAPER DAN

I find myself at a precipice, forty-seven years after I had gone off to war. I have Parkinson's disease that has lain dormant in me until eight years ago and now I spend my waking moments shaking. When I was a young infantry man with the 101st division, I drank water from wherever I could get it. In the hundred-degree heat of Vietnam we could never get enough water. Taking water from streams or out of bomb craters we would treat it with a couple of purification tablets to kill off the water born bacteria, and we thought we were in the clear. By whatever processes I managed to take enough defoliant chemicals into my body to cause problems. I have now undergone DBS surgery to help correct some of the symptoms of the Parkinson's. Three months later my surgery has been a great success. I estimate that my symptoms have been relieved by about ninety percent. It is time that I tell my story.

VIETNAM

My story begins as a 20-year-old kid in Vietnam where they called me Diaper Dan. I had been with the second platoon for nearly eight months. We were part of the 101st Airborne Division (Air Mobil) in Vietnam. I had been packing the PRC-25 (Portable Radio Communication) radio for over six months on mostly platoon and squad size missions in northern I Corps. I learned and became adept at keeping in contact with the tactical operations center (TOC) and other units in our area of operation (AO) and had developed my skills at calling in artillery, gunships, medical evacuation and TAC air.

On about the first of August 1970, word came down that the 1st platoon needed a volunteer to fill a vacancy caused by one of their Radio Telephone Operator's (RTO) being called home for a convalescent leave. I volunteered, with some reluctance, and agreed to leave my platoon to join them in Phu Bia to fill in during the mission that would be taking place while their RTO was absent.

The 1st platoon was understrength when we started the mission. As I recall, we went to the field with twenty-three people including our company commander Captain Arrington, his RTO and Sergeant Muellenbach, as our Platoon Leader. Even though we were understrength some 17 men (40 was a full-time platoon) we were inserted west of Fire Base Bastogne between the Asha Valley and Fire base Ripcord. Our mission, as I understood, it was to probe around the area and pinpoint the location of enemy positions and numbers.

I was on the first bird in the insertion. We landed without firing or receiving any fire. I followed Sgt. Muellenbach to the edge of our LZ where he began to establish a perimeter, and I confirmed communications with the TOC. When our people were all on the ground, we formed up to move along the ridgeline we had landed on. I was at the center of the platoon with the platoon leader and the company commander. We spent the first several days moving around that ridgeline and sending out squad size patrols to gather information and get a feel for what was going on in our area of operation. Within hours we were hearing about trails all over the place and seeing lots of signs of North Vietnamese Army (NVA) activity.

On our third day out, we received resupply late in the afternoon. Upon arrival of the resupply bird, I watched the RTO who I was there to replace step out of the bird. It turned out his convalescent leave had been canceled because of some misinformation discovered before he was able to board a plane for home. As a result, I became an assistant machine gunner for the remainder of the mission.

On our fourth day out, we moved as a platoon down off the ridgeline. The terrain went from scrub brush to a double and triple canopy jungle. Our gun team was just in front of rear security as we made our way down into the canyon. We were seeing enemy sign all around as we made our way. As we approached the bottom of the canyon, we came to a little bit of a stream and a significant trail. A a few yards from where we discovered it, the trail forked. At my position at the rear, by the time I saw the trail, the platoon was strung out down the main trail and the point team was beginning to probe up the fork. Bill

Anderson, who was walking point was maybe thirty yards up the side trail when the first initial shots of an ambush rang out. The front of the platoon hit the ground and began to return fire while the rest of us began to maneuver our position to join our firepower to the rest of the platoon, all this on my first day on the gun team. The jungle was so thick we couldn't see anything but leaves and bark falling from the bullets passing above us through the heavy canopy. We returned fire into the wall of brush in the direction the fire was coming from. Three or four times the firing subsided then with a fury started back up again. During one of the lulls in the firing, I had the bright idea to pitch a grenade. I pulled the pin on a baseball frag and stood up to throw it. I could see the faces of a few of my platoon as I stood, they all had a look of approval. I reared back and gave that frag the mightiest heave I could muster. The highest point of its trajectory was just inches short of the top of the trees that we all hoped it would clear. It tumbled listlessly through the trees and brush about twenty feet to our front as I yelled; "Grenade!" and hit the ground. In my short flight from standing to my stomach, I observed the looks on my comrades' faces. The looks screamed, "What an Idiot!" Everyone ducked as low as they could, and the brush absorbed all the explosion, and no one was hurt by my halfhearted attempt aside from my pride.

At the point we began taking fire, Lieutenant Muellenbach made the call for gunships. As we waited their arrival, we continued to pour some more fire power into the brush. Once all of us were in position, we were able to suppress the oncoming fire from the ambush site and enable the point team to back out of the kill zone. I watched as Bill, our point man had to leave his rucksack to crawl out of the kill zone down a small depression. Several point team members were slightly wounded. Once the gunships arrived on station and were giving the enemy hell, our platoon began making their way back up towards our previous night's position.

We were able to gain the safety of the ridge line where we could call for artillery support, medevac and resupply.
Due to the triple canopy we were unable to see the enemy or much of the effect of the fire from our gunships.
The platoon spent a sleepless night guarding our little perimeter.

The next morning, August 5th, 1970, we moved out to probe down into the same area where contact was made the previous day. We took a roundabout route off the ridge altering our line of march from the day before. Our M-60 moved out with the point team. I walked fourth man behind Jim Blondell, our machine gunner, with a point and slack man going before him. The rest of the platoon was strung out behind us as we moved deeper into the canyon below the ridgeline. As the canopy got thicker the point slowed the pace, we could hear and smell the enemy along with faint metallic sounds that seemed to come from no direction. Sweat and fishy aroma trapped in the layered profusion of leaves and damp soil silently penetrated the lower spaces of the jungle.

We moved silently all through the morning and into the early afternoon. Moving us up a small stream the point man gave us the signal to halt. We took up defensive positions on either side of the small stream. From where I crouched, I could see an NVA helmet and sitting on top of it was a bar of soap, still wet. We could hear voices talking in Vietnamese, relaxed and conversational. My heart was in my throat as we looked around, every particle of each of us searching for where the voices were coming from. We then realized that the voices were coming from some twenty feet above us from a hole in the bank of the stream, concealed by brush. Jim set up the gun to cover the entrance of the fighting position, and I took up a position to his left. The point and slack sat up to our left as we signaled for the M-79 to be brought up. Our M-79 man did a great job of lobbing a grenade directly into the hole; it bounced around inside the hole and didn't go off. Jim opened fire with the M-60. The point and slack took the hole under fire and the two fighting trenches that were previously concealed now became apparent to both sides.

There were six NVA above us within 30 feet with AK-47's trying to get their heads up high enough to bring effective fire down on us. As I crouched next to Jim linking up one belt of ammo after another, he was able to put out a great enough volume of fire to keep their heads down. But he couldn't let up for a second or they were all over us. We had fire superiority, but they had the better position. Each time the gun would jam, or we had to change barrels, I would pick up my M-16 and pour as much fire as possible into the enemy positions. I was in the process of linking up a new belt of ammo when the gun jammed. In that moment I finished the link up and was reaching for my M-16 when an NVA soldier stood up in one of the fighting trenches with an RPG on his shoulder. Time stopped as I tried to bring my weapon to bear. I could see the face of my enemy clearly and see the blossom of the rocket coming out of the tube and the look of satisfaction on his face. My arms felt like lead as the rocket closed the distance between us. I was flying backwards through the air, and Jim was flying too. I remember thinking this is what it is like to die. As I lay on my back looking up, leaves were raining down in small pieces onto my face from the explosion and from the hundreds of rounds of ammunition that were passing over. The explosion had left me momentarily deaf. I looked to my right and saw Jim bleeding but moving. Jim and I both crawled back to the gun and got it firing again. The gun had become so hot that a round cooked off in the feed tray rendering the gun useless. Jim yelled run, and the two of us along with the point and slack were able to back out of the kill zone.

The LT had gun ships waiting for a run at them as soon as we were far enough back to give them a clear shot. Artillery was also called in but was unable to come to bear due to the location of the fighting. Resupply and medivac were called for and several guys were taken out including Jim who had taken some shrapnel from the RPG. I was asked if I needed a medivac, I had powder burns and couldn't hear much but opted not to leave. A new M-60 came out on the resupply, and I became the machine gunner. My assistant gunner was the point man who had lost his ruck sack the day before. As it turned out he only had three days left to serve in country. We regrouped and after the artillery and gunships were done, advanced back into the area we had just fought over. We had two dead NVA and blood trails leading away towards the top of the next ridge. Our point lead us to the top of the ridge where we took a break. It was now getting on towards late afternoon. A Loach flew over with some brass in it and radioed down that he had seen some NVA moving down the ridge we were on. Our platoon leaders, Sgt. Muellenbach and Captain Arrington, informed us that we would be moving out down the ridgeline in pursuit of the fleeing NVA. I said to Sgt. Muellenbach, "Sir, it's late in the day, and we should wait till tomorrow and probe into that valley from another direction." He said, "Take your gun to the rear of the column." I thought his reaction a little odd but proceeded with my assistant gunner to move my gun to take up a position with rear security. At this point our platoon was down to 13 men.

The point team led off down the ridge with Sgt. Muellenbach, walking just behind the front gun team. My gun was bringing up the rear. A break was called for, and I sat down facing backward, covering the trail we had just come down. My assistant gunner stepped off the trail to relieve himself just as a message came up the line. Send up a LAW, send up a LAW (light antitank weapon). As I looked down the trail, I could see under the brush that it intersected with an even larger trail and that there were wheel tracks from a French 51 antiaircraft gun on that trail. I'm thinking, "Man, we shouldn't be here," when the front gun opens up. I heard six rounds clear the gun when there was a series of explosions. Smoke and dust rose out of the jungle and up the trail. Someone was yelling, "Get the gun up here. Get the other gun up here!" I headed down the trail with my gun as fast as I could leaving my Assistant gunner to catch up as he could. Smoke was drifting through the jungle where the bottom of the ridge spilled into a fairly flat area. Small arms fire was constant but not well directed coming our way. I sat the gun up in a circle of Teakwood trees and directed some of the walking wounded to take up defensive positions. Just then my AG shows up and says to me, "Dan, I can't go up there." You just didn't ask a guy with three days left to go expose himself in that way. So, he took over the gun. I took his M-16 and made my way up toward the point. Guys were moving back to our perimeter, and I was able to direct several of them in the right direction. The trail they had come down was daisy-chained, (a series of mines set up as an ambush). Everyone had been hit except for me and my AG. On my second trip up towards the point, I reached the captain. He was laying against a tree trunk along with his RTO. Both were covered with blood. I was able to get the RTO headed back to our little perimeter and call for support. The captain looked bad. He kept telling me to check Sgt. Muellenbach's pulse. Over and over he said, "Check his pulse." The sergeant was missing both legs, one arm and the other arm was attached by a thread. I placed my fingers on his neck where a pulse should have been and said, "He's dead, sir." We rolled his torso into a poncho and dragged him back to the perimeter.

By this time there was a medivac pulling guys out using a jungle penetrator. Several of the walking wounded gave mouth to mouth to the gunner. I too took a turn at keeping him breathing. One of the claymores had blown bits of purple smoke grenade into his lungs. Each breath that we gave him ignited the fragments of grenade (white phosphorous) so that he exhaled smoke and the smell of burning tissue. In between breaths he spoke of home and his Mom. We tied him to the jungle penetrator (an airlift that hung from the Huey), and I remember that he was still alive as he was drawn up out of the jungle.

I made one more trip out of the perimeter into the kill zone to see if anyone was left behind. I saw an M-16 that was laying out in the open. From my place of concealment behind a giant teakwood tree, I could see that it had been blown in half. It was getting dark but as I looked around, I spotted nine bunkers with people moving around like ants on an ant hill.

I got back to our little perimeter just as my AG was loading the last walking wounded onto the penetrator. We kept running to the gun position and putting out rounds to make the enemy think we were able to keep up the fight. 23 soldiers had turned into two, and all that was left was me, my AG, our weapons, radio and about thirty-five pounds of the sergeant in a body bag. We had been using a strobe light to guide the medivac to our hole in the jungle, but as we moved back and forth between getting guys on the medivac and our fighting positions, we either lost it or it went dead or the previous lift took it with him.

It was pure dark, so we tried to guide the extraction Huey into us with a flash light. We could hear him hovering right above us and sometimes caught a bit of his silhouette through the trees. He turned on his search light to try and find us and immediately came under fire from an antiaircraft gun. He had to pull out. The tracers from the antiaircraft looked like fiery pumpkins reaching for him. The volume of small arms fire from the enemy had fallen off. We put on our rucksacks, picked up our weapons, grabbed the body bag between us and hauled ass out of there back up the hill we had come down. As we neared the top of the ridge, the terrain began to open up and enough starlight filtered through the canopy that we were able to find our way. We found a huge dense brushy area at the backbone of the ridge and began to burrow into it dragging our equipment and the body bag with us. We burrowed and turned and burrowed some more until we were at the apex of the ridge near the center of the brush pile. We laid quiet for a while listening while the sounds around us returned to normal.

Small animals began to make their night sounds, and the night birds resumed their calls. My heart was pounding so hard; I was afraid the enemy could hear it from fifty feet away. Finally, I was able to calm down from the adrenaline rush of the last several hours. I could smell the remains in the body bag we had dragged with us, and I hoped it did not permeate far enough for the enemy to pick up on it. After laying down for maybe half an hour, we began to hear the sounds of the NVA in the general direction from which we had entered the brush pile. As the sounds drew closer, we could hear specific commands and response to those commands. The NVA tried to set the brush on fire. We saw a few little flashes of light, but the brush was too wet to burn. After a while, the sounds began to move away. We would communicate with each other in a low whisper. We agreed that even a Super Gook was not crazy enough to get down on his belly and crawl into this burrow in the middle of the night. Even so, one of us sat with his weapon trained on our back trail the whole time.

By midnight we had heard no nearby signs of the enemy. It had been several hours. I got on the radio and tried to reestablish communications. I was able to reach the TOC right away. The problem was that before I could give them our location, I could hear at least one strange radio come onto our frequency. That was a good indication that the NVA were listening in and if they could stay with us long enough, could triangulate to get our position. Every time I would hear them come on, I would say, Charley, Mike, Delta, Hotel, Charley, One. This was our code to change up or down the dial to a different frequency. By doing this over and over and coding the message, I was able to report our position accurately and let the rear know of our status. Near two AM we got a message from the TOC that there was a LURP team a little over a klick away from us on our same ridge line. They were on route to link up with us. These were some great guys. We laid quietly in the brush waiting for them until around 0400.

The small animal noises disappeared around us. We strained to decipher the slightest sound. We had been in communication with the LURP team for about an hour and were breaking squelch every fifteen minutes, as a sign that everything was all clear. Clouds had moved in casting us into a darker shade of blackness. I turned the volume on my radio down as low as I could and took the hand set away from my ear. I could hear squelch break in the brush about ten feet away. I whispered, "Diaper Dan", back came, "LURP Team."

The morning of the sixth broke clear. We stayed hid in our brush pile until we had plotted artillery strikes around us and our extraction helicopter was in bound. We packed our remaining gear and the body bag and boarded one of the helicopters that was bringing in the company that was there to replace us. As we boarded, a fresh-looking LT asked one of the LURPs. Seen any Gooks? I will never forget his reply, "Plenty in the canyons, Sir."

Our entire battalion had been pulled out of the field the day before. When our bird landed at Phu Bai, I said good bye to the LURPs and rode in a jeep to the company area along with the AG. He was down to two days in country, so he began processing out. The company area was all but deserted. A company clerk told me to go straight to the parade field for a battalion formation. At the formation I was the only member of first platoon. So, there was this platoon size hole in the formation with just me in it.

I was filthy and stinking from the mission standing there in the late morning sun listening to the same officer who had ordered us into that valley drone on about the success of the mission and what a great job we had all done. When he was done speaking, another officer took over to tell us what would be happening for the next week that the battalion would be out of the field. The battalion commander made his way directly to me as the other officer continued to speak. When he was about two steps from me, he stopped and addressed me personally. To this day I couldn't tell you the words that were coming out of his mouth. I just wanted to scream, grab him and throw him down on his back and ask him why the hell he ordered us down into that canyon at that time of day. It was the wrong thing to do on so many levels. I was ready to unleash my fury on him when Jim walked up (the machine gunner I had replaced). The colonel turned his attention to him. Just then the formation was dismissed, and the guys from my regular platoon saw me and called out. "Hey Diaper Dan, you made it!"

The last time anyone called me Diaper Dan was over forty years ago. Since then I have been a fisherman from the Yukon River to La Paz, Mexico. I have been a carpenter in California, Oregon and Alaska. I've had numerous adventures and met enough colorful characters to fill the pages of several books. It is my desire to pass onto my children and grandchildren as many of my experiences as I can before passing from this earth.

To place this story in time I would have to take you back to 1968. I was about to graduate from high school. My brother Kit and cousin Gary had joined the Air Force to fulfill their military duty and avoid the possibility of having to serve on the ground in Vietnam. That was the totality of my awareness of the war. I didn't watch a lot of TV or discuss the war with my friends. It was out there in the background, but I was too involved with bending my Honda through a curve, going to the beach, or contemplating a party next weekend to give it any serious thought. I had been inoculated with the words of Nikita Khrushchev when he banged his shoe on the gavel in front of the whole world and said, "We will bury you," and by getting under our desks to cover our heads to survive the nuke that was almost sure to come. Little did I know that I was about to experience the words of our president who said, "Ask not what your country can do for you but what you can do for your country."

PART ONE

SURFING IN MEXICO

Near the end of my senior year in high school, I was in an art class with Dwight Graham and Ron Jensen. They were both experienced surfers and well known for their skills around Santa Cruz. We were working on a project together, a poster for an upcoming game, I think. As we worked, they were talking about a trip to Mexico to go surfing. All they needed was a vehicle capable of the trip. I had recently traded my Honda Super-hawk for a 1952 GMC window panel and chimed in that I might be available to make the trip. The three of us walked out of class and straight to the school parking lot to inspect my ride and seal the deal. I was a strong swimmer and had spent many a day at the beach. I'd body surfed and belly boarded a bit but had very little experience with a surf board. Dwight and Ron assured me that they could come up with a board for me and teach me how to use it. We agreed that we should each have at least three hundred dollars to make the trip and began to make it our goal to have it together before school let out for the summer.

We departed Santa Cruz in the morning a few days after school let out and drove down the coast as far as Santa Barbara. There we slept the night in the van outside some kind of monastery. Ron wanted to check in with his spiritual guru before heading out, so Dwight and I spent the morning hours cooling our heels while Ron topped off his spiritual tank. We headed for the border about noon and crossed the border just after dark at Mexicali. We continued to drive through the night pulling over far out in the desert to sleep for a few hours. After we pulled off the road all was quiet; it was hot in the panel. Ron decided he was going to sleep outside. The night sounds of the coyotes weren't strange to us, but the rattles of the snakes brought Ron back inside after a short time. The next morning, we were back on the road when the sun came up. Late morning, I was driving along another seemingly endless, straight stretch of two lanes. Dwight had taken to riding on top of the rig, sitting in the sun on one of the surfboards fastened to the rack. I noticed a funky looking sign at the side of the road hand lettered in Spanish. Seconds later I could see the road was missing for a space of fifty or sixty feet where an empty creek bed passed under it. I slammed on the brakes to avoid pitching into the abyss. Dwight, clinging to my surfboard came flying off the roof, smacked the hood and disappeared over the front. We had come to a halt with my front wheels about three feet from the edge of the missing bridge. Ron and I jumped out of the truck to find Dwight with the board under his arm making his way up out of the dry creek bed. It was a good twenty vertical feet from the road surface to the rocks below, plus the six or so feet to the top of the panel. Dwight managed to land on the only sandy spot available in his flight from the truck, a testament to his physical condition and good luck. We strapped the board back onto the rack and backtracked to the sign that by now we ascertained said detour or bridge out. After a short drive out through the desert through the rocks and cactus, we were back on the road. Vowing that if we saw another such road sign, we would stop and translate it before moving on.

Somewhere in the desert, north of Los Mochas, the truck began to over heat and run rough. I pulled off the road under an abandoned bridge into the only shade available. We had to let the thing cool down before removing the radiator cap to check the coolant. Ron spotted a Gila monster on the bridge abutment about ten feet away from the right front fender. It did not seem to be bothered by our presence and made no effort to leave during the hour or so that we were there. I removed the thermostat to allow the coolant to circulate more freely and refilled the radiator with water that we carried with us. The spark plugs were fouled from the questionable gas south of the border, so I cleaned them up as best I could and made a note to buy a new set as soon as possible. Ron and Dwight were taken aback by my mechanical skills and quite satisfied at their decision to include me on this adventure. Several hours later we were pulling into Los Mochas, looking for an auto parts store. We found what we were looking for on a dirt street in a seedy part of the outskirts of town. Ron and Dwight watched over the truck as I pulled a spark plug to match up to the ones that were for sale. Upon exiting the parts store there were six or more young Mexican males near the front of the truck. Ron was inside with the doors locked and just the front passenger window rolled down. Dwight was at the front bumper taking my tools back from various members of the group as fast as they could pick them up to look at them. I climbed up on the fender and began to change out the plugs, while keeping one eye on the drama unfolding around me. One of the locals made a kick at Dwight, the smile never left Dwight's face as he blocked the kick with his foot and delivered one of his own sending the instigator back on his ass. The rest of the bunch got smiles on their faces and the whole atmosphere got friendly as Dwight spoke to them in Spanish and shared with them some of his martial arts expertise. The auto parts store had a sand blaster for cleaning spark plugs, so I had them cleaned for a spare set when we got under way.

Our next stop was Mazatlán, where we checked into a hotel near the beach that had a gated garage, so we didn't have to guard the truck. Ron and Dwight couldn't wait to go surfing. After a few sets came through, Ron took the time to school me on some of the rudiments of surfing. We spent two nights there exploring the area around our hotel. It was the first time I'd ever seen real organized beggars that would pursue you down the street and try to corner you. There were some scary parts of that city where young gringos were fair game.

It was good to be back on the road headed for San Blas. The land had gone from desert to jungle like passing through a curtain. We pulled into San Blas late in the afternoon. The woman who ran the Flamingo hotel in the middle of town said that she had a house that we could rent in a couple of days. She booked us into the hotel in the interim. There were four guys from Texas getting ready to leave town in a couple of days that would be vacating the place we would call home for the next two months. We spent the next several days checking out the beaches and the jungle and getting to know our way around San Blas. By walking our boards out to the point at the north end of the bay we could paddle out and catch a wave that would carry us over a mile up the bay to a hotel that sat at the edge of the jungle there. One of us would drive the panel down the beach to the hotel and sit inside or out on the beach with a cold drink until the others surfed their way down the bay to the hotel. Then we would switch drivers and repeat the process. Each cycle took about an hour and a half depending on how the waves were breaking.

In the afternoon the wind chop would come up and there were some big sharks that cruised through at that time. Out on the plantations the mosquitos would get bad driving the workers back into town where the smoke from cooking kept them at bay. Tradition called for siesta at that time, and we soon fell into that practice.

Before leaving Santa Cruz, we had made numerous trips to Goodwill and other used clothing establishments. We purchased all the aloha type shirts we could find to wear and to use for trade goods. This kept us from having to do laundry. When we had worn a shirt for a couple of days it was traded away, off our backs, for whatever we needed, mostly food or beer. We had also brought baseball gear and would get it out in the afternoons to put together a game of workups in the street in front of our house. As far as I know we had the only real baseballs, bats, and gloves in the town. This drew kids and young men from all around to get involved. As a result, we became popular guests at weekend cookouts and barbeques.

JAGUARS AND PEYOTE

Most of the residents of San Blas had no refrigeration in 1968, so they butchered large animals on Friday night or Saturday morning. The meat would be parceled out to family and friends and consumed before it could go bad. As a result, we enjoyed the hospitality of our baseball crew most weekends. We always showed up with balls and bats and beer. There was one Mexican surfer, named John, that we met at the beach who would ride in the truck with us back to the point. John became our friend and introduced us to his family who ran a plantation a few miles up the river from San Blas, growing bananas, pineapples, tomatoes and more. Their farm could be reached by road when the weather was dry for an extended period, but was most commonly reached by boat. There was a launch that ran up the river several times a day to service the farms and a restaurant that sat in the jungle along the river. One day, we all loaded up and rode the launch up the river and met John at the plantation. After a tour of the grounds and a great homemade dinner, the four of us retired to a small cabin that sat at the edge of a band of jungle and ran between the river and a field of banana trees. John told us not to stray far from the cabin because the jaguars hunted near the farm at night. We took this with a grain of salt as we played cards by the flickering oil lamp. There was a point in the night while we were all awake when the jungle around us went completely quiet. From out of the night came a low growl, effortless, like a cat's purr only it carried like the echo in a tunnel. I wasn't as quick to step outside to pee for the rest of the night, and as I lay on my pallet to sleep, awoke several times to hear that same low growl. Once before dawn we were all awakened by a much louder roar and growl. From the other side of the room I heard John say, "The cat has found his dinner." Rain greeted us the next morning, but by the time we had breakfast, the boat was there to pick us up, and the sun was out. It was a beautiful scene with the trees cloaked in mist at the bottom and sun shining through their tops.

We had been planning a trip to Guadalajara to visit the biggest marketplace in Mexico. On the day we had planned, I came down with the dreaded Montezuma's Revenge. Ron and Dwight boarded a bus for there after a trip to the pharmacy for the local cure for me. I spent the day close to home. At around six that evening the two of them rolled up in the bus with bags full of stuff they had purchased and traded for. What they had to share with me was a bottle of Tequila with a worm in it and some horrible stuff called Peyote. They explained to me that if I chewed the peyote fast then drank a swig of tequila, then licked some salt off my hand then bit into some lime, I would not only be cured from the Montezuma's revenge but be feeling much, much better. After three or four cycles of the cure, I still wasn't feeling any better, so Ron and Dwight headed a few steps down the street to the Torino Bar and Café to have dinner. Not long after they departed, I began to feel much better and headed in that direction myself. Upon entering the bar, I spotted Ron and Dwight at a table near the alligator pit that sat in the corner of the bar. One of Dwight's methods of entertaining us was to grab a gator by the tail and give it a shake before one of his cousins could lunge for Dwight's hand. Of course, this activity was much enhanced by the consumption of tequila, peyote and now beer. By the time my hand reached for the nearest available tail the gators were all warmed up for the game. I felt the snout of one of the oily buggers brush the back of my fingers as I withdrew my hand from his compatriot's tail. Having participated in that and hearing all the room wince at my near miss I decided to stick my head into the café portion of the establishment. Upon doing so I caught the eye of the doctor. I had met him several days before down on the beach. He and his wife and daughter were traveling for several months in Mexico with Rosa their babysitter and all-around helper. The Doc waved me over to the table and explained that there was a dance contest going on at that moment in the restaurant and that Rosa had no dance partner. The suggestion that I enter a dance contest was working its way through my tequila and peyote addled brain when Rosa got to her feet and swept me onto the dance floor. The next half hour was a whirl of rock and roll mariachi with the couples around us being eliminated one by one. Rosa and I danced like we had been practicing together for weeks. A balloon was suspended between us as we rocked and swayed, and the crowd clapped and cheered us on. As the song came to an end there was but one other couple beside us on the floor. The winners would be decided by the applause of the crowd. Rosa and I were by far the favorites. Rosa was hugging me, and I relished the attention from her and the adulation of the crowd. Just then, a voice in Spanish rose above the noise of the throng. Rosa looked at me with hurt and disappointment in her eyes. "You did not pay your entry fee!" she said. "I came in through the bar," was my reply. As six pairs of Mexican hands propelled me towards the door,

I felt myself being swung like a sack of potatoes through the air. The lights of the Torino Café whirled above me as the cobble stone street glistened from an evening rain. I hoped for a landing that would not include stitches. Several seconds later as I picked myself up, some of the locals who had launched me stood under the awning at the front of the café still taunting me. I recognized several Spanish curse words that I had only recently become familiar with. I made my way back to the house where Ron and Dwight joined me an hour or so later. We sat up and had one last drink of tequila and laughed about the day.

Our next adventure found Dwight and I at the boat harbor where the river flows into the sea. We had been fishing for our dinner and talking to one of the locals we had come to be acquainted with through baseball. He had several boats. One was a modern fiberglass and the other an old original dug-out about twenty feet long. He said we could use the old canoe the next day as long as we would take along with us his two nephews who would be in town on vacation from their school in Guadalajara. We met up with the boys the following day at the harbor. The two boys, who I would guess to be fourteen, were dressed in their school uniforms, flat brimmed straw hats, tan shorts with matching shirts, black shoes, socks and ties. After being introduced and being warned not to go beyond the rocks that sat a few hundred yards beyond the mouth of the harbor, we loaded some fishing gear into the canoe and were off. At the river's mouth Dwight and I jumped into the chest deep water and pushed the canoe over the bar and into the blue Pacific. Dwight was in the front and I in the back as we paddled towards the rocks with our passengers. Dwight spoke to them in Spanish as we got out the poles and started to fish. The gentle current would pull us past the rocks as we fished carrying us away from the mouth of the river and we would paddle back each time picking up a couple of sea perch or rock bass at each tour pass the rocks.

The boys had big grins as they caught their share of fish, and we were enjoying being their fishing guides. A little after noon, it must have been about high slack tide. The ocean was calm, it was hot with barely a breath of breeze. We had just paddled back to the north end of the rocks. Dwight eased over the side to cool off, as we had been doing alternately all morning. The two students were still fully uniformed up. I guess they were just used to it. Dwight was swimming, perhaps fifty feet in front of the canoe. As I looked past him, I noticed a large dorsal fin about a hundred yards away moving in our direction. Calling out to Dwight, I made him aware of the situation prompting him to re-enter the canoe. Within a few minutes, there were five large sharks milling around the area surrounding the canoe. Two large manta rays joined them, and it seemed as though we were at the center of a SeaWorld show. At this point we pulled all our fishing gear, considering it prudent not to introduce any more blood or attractants into the water. The largest of the sharks, easily as long as our craft, was cruising just under the surface pushing up a swell in front of him and headed straight for the middle of the canoe. Our students became extremely agitated, so much so that the one in front stood up in the canoe, waving his arms and threatening the balance of the craft. Dwight pulled his feet out from under him plopping him down on his ass and administered a couple of karate slaps, bringing both students under control and stability back to our canoe. As this was taking place, my eyes were glued to the shark and its huge wide head and mouth as it passed under the boat. I imagined myself wedged between the sides of the overturned canoe as the students were thrown into the drink with the five sharks making passes at them in their uniforms. When I came out of my daydream the shark's tail was passing beneath the boat just under me. At this point the sharks and the mantas began to circle the canoe at about fifteen yards out in a nice orderly fashion. We began to paddle towards shore in as calm a manner as we could muster. Our sharks continued to circle us as we made for the nearest point of shore. We had drifted south perhaps a half mile from the mouth of the river. Guiding us in to about a foot of water, Dwight and I got out of the canoe on the shoreward side and pushed it toward the entrance to the harbor. As we bounced it along in the shallow water, we could still see the shadows of the great beasts as they continued to parallel our movements, following us until we were once more inside the harbor. We delivered our passengers to the dock side where they talked excitedly with their uncle. He had a good laugh over their stories. We went home with about half the fish we caught leaving the remainder to be sold or traded by the boat owner.

A couple of days after our fishing adventure Ron and Dwight were hot to go to a place called Punta de Mita. They explained to me that it was a famous surfing spot, visited only by a few surfers because of its remote location. We could reach it in a day's travel, about forty miles of which would be dirt roads. We headed south again towards Puerto Vallarta. We reached the turn off to Punte de Mita at about noon, and the track turned immediately to dirt. In places the road split then came back together with itself, leading us to wonder if we were going the right way. The terrain alternated between desert and jungle as we made our way mostly in first and second gear. At one point the road ran into a creek and did not come out on the opposite bank. By wading up the creek with me in the panel, Dwight discovered that the road was the creek bed for about a quarter of a mile before climbing the bank once more. I followed a set of tractor wheel marks up the bank and we found ourselves in a cluster of palm roofed shacks with a few pigs running about. I pulled to a stop in front of one of the shacks and shut the truck down. We called through the open windows, "Ola!" There was a commotion in the shack nearest to us and the side of it opened up into an awning. Inside were several Mexican women who offered to make drinks for us made out of coconut. Kid's swarmed out of the other shacks along with more women and soon we were being offered beans and tortillas to go with our drinks. I saw a fifty-gallon drum and asked if I could buy some gas. Pulling over next to the drum, a woman pumped my tank full. Just as she had finished with the gas, a herd of horses came running in from the direction we were going. Each horse carried a man and each man a machete. They were loud and waved their machetes in the air as they surrounded and milled around the truck. Ron and I did a lot of smiling and nodding as Dwight began to speak to them. It turned out they were just coming in for lunch, and we were already eating their lunch when they showed up. All of them got down and tied their horses as more drinks and food were brought out. From somewhere a record player started to crank out Mexican music as we sat and ate and drank under the trees. After an hour or so we drove on with about ten Mexican Cowboys on our running boards and fenders. When we came to a Y in the road the cowboys left us to go back to work, and we proceeded towards Punta de Mita. Nearing the point, we drove through a desert landscape in view of the ocean. One thing I remember was that each time we stopped, land crabs appeared to rush out to do battle with the truck tires. Later we realized the reason. Each time we stopped, we would see them creep towards the truck to feed on their friends who were recently crushed.

The only structure at Punta de Mita was a colorfully painted concrete building that sat between the ocean and a runway, big enough for small planes. There was one guy there holding down the fort. He had warm beer for sale and a single surfboard to rent. Dwight talked to him for a few minutes, and we were off to check out the waves. I pulled the truck up a couple of miles from the airport out on a point with waves breaking all around. We found a sandy spot several hundred yards from the water, where there were no land crabs, as a spot to camp for the night. We got the boards down off the rack and headed for the water. The rocks near the water were covered with barnacles, very rough on the feet. It was necessary to thread your way between the rocks in the sandy areas to get out to deep enough water to get on our boards. As I did so, I could see thousands of sea urchins that had to be avoided to keep from stepping on their sharp spines. I reached waist deep water before getting on my board and beginning to paddle. I thought I was seeing things at first when it seemed, the bottom was moving away from me. It was thousands of stingrays. The bottom in the shallows inside of the reef was covered with them. By this time Ron and Dwight had paddled outside and were catching waves. I realized this place was too dangerous for my skill range. If I was to fall off my board and put my foot down on a stingray or sea urchins, none of us would be having any more fun. I paddled around for a bit checking out the sea life inside the reef. It was like some kind of marine sanctuary. Getting back to the truck I rounded up some wood for a camp fire and enjoyed the sunset. Dwight and Ron got in just before dark. We ate fruit, canned beans and tortillas and watched the stars come out. The next day we drove the truck up and down the point stopping at every new break to surf. There were a couple of places sandy enough for me to try it out, but for the most part it was Ron and Dwight's show.

In the early afternoon Ron stepped on a sea urchin. Five or six spines had broken off deep up in his instep. He was in great pain, so we decided to drive to Puerto Vallarta to get him to a doctor. We left Punta de Mita around four in the afternoon and drove without stopping until reaching a small clinic after dark. The doctor there was able to treat Ron's foot and relieve some of his pain. Dwight and I decided to drive back to our house in San Blas that night. After driving for several hours, we stopped at a road house on a mountain pass. As we were eating, I asked a guy at the next table, what time it was. I didn't think he heard me, so I asked him again, and then a third time. Next thing you know he's pissed off, cursing me in Spanish. He pulled back the lapel on his jacket to let me know he was packing an ivory handled chrome 45 auto. I had been thinking up to that point that my Spanish was getting better. We paid our tab and got back to the truck headed north. Ron was sleeping for the first time, so we just drove until the truck was almost out of gas. We found a gas station and slept in the truck till it opened in the morning. From there it was only a couple of hours back to San Blas.

John, a local surfer, had a sister, Maria, who owned a small beach shop in town. Maria was in her mid-twenties and easy to talk to. She spoke excellent English and was very helpful. In telling her about our run-in with the guy up on the mountain pass, she said we were very lucky. Few people drive that stretch of road at night because of bandits. We had just about enough money between us to buy gas to get back home. After being gone for over two months and with Ron still limping, we headed north. Stopping only for breaks to change drivers, we made it back to Santa Cruz in record time.

I dropped off Ron and Dwight down by Opal Cliffs and made it to Scotts Valley at about noon or so. When I pulled up to the house, Dad and Mom had the truck, trailer and car packed and were ready to head out to move the family to Oregon. I made a pass through the Shell gas station, where I had been working before leaving for Mexico, to get the remainder of a final pay check that I had coming from the owner, J C Miller. While I was there, he offered me my old job back, and I accepted. I drove the two blocks to our place on Vine Hill Road and said good-bye to my family. The house was sold, but Dad let me have the keys to the shop on the adjoining property where I could stay until it sold. I was on my own.

THE BULL RIDE

The Shell station, where I worked, sat at the corner of Scotts Valley Drive and Glenwood Road, within a hundred yards of the overpass to Highway 17. One of the guys working there, in the fall of 1968, was named Greg. He and I pulled the same shifts together fairly regularly. Greg drove a late model Malibu that he kept in mint condition. He was a good guy to work with always doing his share and a little more. While talking during the slow hours of a Friday night into Saturday morning, we got on the subject of rodeo. Somehow or another I managed to say that I wouldn't mind trying to ride one of them bulls. Like I was saying, Greg is a squared away guy, buttoned down; his mom was still doing his laundry, but he wasn't a bull-shitter. He says, "Hey Ken, come and check this out." He was standing in the illumination provided by his trunk light. I walked over and looked down into his neat as a pin trunk. There on the carpet was a coil of leather rope with some kind of leather hand grip sewn on it along with some leather gloves. Behind those close to the front of the trunk was a pair of chaps and a crisp new straw cowboy hat. "Ever seen a bull riding rig before?" Greg Inquired. "Ah! Ah! No." Greg closed the trunk, and we walked back over into the station lights.

44

A customer pulled into the pumps dinging the air bell mounted on the wall by the first mechanical bay. Another car drove into the island behind him bringing the fog with him. A wave of "Fill her up's" and "two dollars' worth" kept the bell ringing in the swirling fog. When things slowed down again, Greg invited me to come out to the fairgrounds in Watsonville. There would be some bulls to ride, and some of the local cowboys would be there. Kind of like a practice for a real rodeo. That next day I met Greg out at the rodeo grounds. He introduced me around as his gas station buddy. I spent a couple of hours back behind the chutes looking at the bulls, the horses, following Greg around and hearing the talk that goes on before the ride. Greg was getting ready to ride a bull and asked me if I would like to take his place. Damn, standing behind the fence and talking is one thing; climbing over that fence and into the chute is another. I climbed up the fence next to Greg and looked down at that bull, and I knew I was not going to try and ride him. Greg had a big grin on his face as he said to me, "I can't let you ride my bull." I watched him ride his bull the full eight seconds. I really don't remember much about the ride just that he stayed on, and the other cowboys who were in on the joke seemed to have big shit eating grins.

THE DONKEY

The shop at Vine Hill Road sold so I moved in with Roger Roesner who lived in his mother's garage. I also spent nights at the Trombles in Lockhart Gulch and with any of my friends and family that would have me. My grandparents had moved out of their home in Felton and let me rent their house, so I had my first real dwelling place. I had a pickup truck, a motorcycle and a place of my own. I was filling in at the gas station and working for my uncle Darby in his construction company. In late winter of 1968 I met George Swenson and went to work for him. He was a contractor and an amazing carpenter who had a real gift for teaching his skills to others. He had a number of jobs going around the Santa Cruz area, but the one I spent the most time on was up Trout Gulch. I helped George build a camp for kids there. We put in a foundation for the main structure first. The owner decided to have horses for the camp, so I got the job of fencing and cross fencing the thirty-acre property. When I wasn't doing that, I was helping George with building the barn and horse corral/arena. The first animal to show up was a burro named

Hee-Haw. He came with a pack saddle and gear to help me move fencing materials around the property. I could load him up with all kinds of stuff, and he would let me lead him anywhere. He would wait as quiet as can be munching on whatever was handy while I cleared out old fence and put in new. He had been my work companion and pal for over a week prior to the first time I rode him. Well, perhaps rode is a bit of an overstatement. It was a Friday afternoon, so I would have to bring in all the tools so as not to leave them out over the weekend. By placing the tools on the branch of a nearby oak tree I was able to mount Hee-Haw and ride him over under the tree. There we paused, and I proceeded to place the posthole digger, bow saw and shovel on my left shoulder. Taking the reins in my right hand, I gave Hee-Haw a slight nudge to let him know we could proceed to the barn. He took several steps towards the barn before starting to buck. It is an amazing realization to witness how high that docile little burro could throw me and my load of tools. At the apex of my upward flight I realized that the bow saw, posthole digger and shovel were somewhere up over my head. Coming down, my rear met with Hee-Haw's rear coming up again. This gave me added momentum to meet up with the posthole digger, bow saw and shovel that were coming back down. The bow saw nearly cut my ear off as the posthole digger's double blades struck the top of my head. I came to with Hee-Haw quietly munching grass a few feet from my head. I could hear George calling for me to come on in; it's time to call it a day. Hee-Haw let me load the tools back on him and lead him back to the barn. I never again suggested that he carry both me and the tools.

THE THOROUGHBRED

As spring broke into summer Roger came to work with us at the Trout Gulch job. Hee-Haw was joined by twelve horses from a ranch up in Oregon where they hadn't been ridden for several years. Exercising and trying to train the horses became a second job for Roger and me. There was one large thoroughbred gelding in the bunch. He hadn't been gelded till after he was two years old. The owner wanted him ridden and trained bareback, so that his 12-year-old daughter could have an equitation horse. I made several attempts to stay on him bareback and was unable to accomplish that. By saddling him and slowly riding him to the bottom of the hill near the entry gate, I could let him run up the hill to the barn. That would take enough of the starch out of him that I could work with him. One evening as I was repeating this maneuver, unbeknownst to me, the owner had pulled up at the gate just as I had started to run the gelding up the hill. When I reached the corral, the owner was right behind. Stepping out of his Lincoln dressed in riding clothes, he said to me, "I thought I told you that I only wanted the gelding ridden bareback." He was not interested in hearing my explanation about not being able to stay on his back. Leading the gelding into the corral and stripping the saddle off, he continued to belittle my efforts as I gave him a boost up to get on the gelding's back. I got to say he did look good on the gelding in his boots and jodhpurs holding his riding quirt. He had the style of a real equestrian, a tall man on a fine-looking horse, trained in the English tradition. He gave a slight movement to the quirt, and the gelding began to move forward. I was prepared to see the gelding put through his paces. At a second twitch of the quirt the gelding bolted straight for the opposite side of the corral in a full-out running buck. The owner did a masterful job of remaining seated until reaching a point about ten feet from the newly constructed timber fence. At that point the gelding planted all four feet and put his head down. The owner left the back of that horse in a flat trajectory like he had been fired from a rifle directly at the top of a 6x6 post where it joined two 2x8's that were part of the top rail. His long body in flight lay crumpled on the ground like a stomped-on accordion. Dipping through the rails I ran to where the owner was in the process of untangling himself from his predicament. I had to shoo the gelding away. He wanted to sniff up close to smell the aroma of defeat on his latest victim. The man would not allow me to help him to his feet but pulled himself erect hoisting on the fence rails. He held himself up, bent at the waist while he waited for his breathing to return to normal. His clothing was dusty, and dirt clung to his sweat as he wavered there in the heat of the corral. His words to me were, "You just gentle him down by whatever methods you deem appropriate." Upon seeing the man a few weeks later, I expressed my doubts that the gelding would ever be a suitable equitation horse for his daughter.

WHERE IT ALL BEGAN

I'm Kenneth Frederic. I was born at Sisters Hospital in Santa Cruz, California on September fourth, nineteen forty-nine. At the time my parents, Oscar and Betty, lived in a small house in Glen

Arbor about ten miles up the San Lorenzo River from the Monterey Bay. Little did I know then how the San Lorenzo Valley, its river, mountains and redwoods, would play such a role in the forming of my character.

My first memories took place in a farm house that sat where the Los Gatos court house now stands. It was a warm morning in the Santa Clara valley. My older brother, Kit, was at kindergarten, and my baby sister, Kathy, was down for a nap. Mom had wrung clothes through a wringer washer set up on a platform next to a shed in the back yard. Between the house and the shed stood a large pepper tree whose trunk sprung from the ground near the back porch. By climbing onto the railing of the porch, I could climb into the tree and make my way out onto the branches that hung near where mom did the wash. On this particular day, the sap was visible between the bark of the tree. Somehow, I managed to transfer some sap from the branches to my eyes. Tears filled my eyes, and I began to cry. I became disoriented being able to see light above and earth below through a screen of tears and leaves. I screamed and cried for Mom.

One of a family of seven depression raised kids, Mom didn't come unglued by the sounds emanating from a truculent three years old. As she went about her work, she warned me to keep my fingers out of my eyes and let the tears wash away the pepper. She assured me that she would not be climbing up the tree to help me, and if I fell to the ground, I should endeavor to land on my head so as to do as little damage as possible.

After crying for a while longer, I began to calm down and work at the strategy Mom had laid out for me. As the tears washed away the burning, my vision began to return. Once I began to feel OK, I climbed farther out on the limb, being careful not to put my hands near my face. Mom finished the wash and hung it to dry. She warned me about falling asleep in the tree before going into the house. I stayed in the tree for a while enjoying the shade and the occasional turn of a light breeze. It occurred to me that falling asleep was a bad idea. I climbed back down to the house where Mom washed my face and gave me a peanut butter sandwich and Koolaid.

Our house sat well back from the road, the drive lined with large trees planted in the early 1900's. They arched over the drive in pairs. At the road stood two palms, then walnuts, avocados and loquats. One driveway went to the back where the barns, chicken house and sheds were located.   The other came straight at the house then turned to join the other drive making a circular drive in the front. This was all part of an old family orchard that spread over ten or more acres. On the farm were apricots, prunes, peaches, walnuts and figs. Our family rented the house and a couple of sheds. The rest was used by the owner and his work force. Unless the areas between the trees were being ploughed or sprayed, we had the run of all of it. One of our favorite places was the fig orchard. The fig trees grew much taller than the cots or prunes. The pickers only picked as far up as the ladders could reach. The tops of the trees grew together forming places where we could climb up one tree then move from tree to tree over quite a large area. My brother Kit and I along with our friends Kerry and Mappy spent many hours in nothing but a pair of shorts being Tarzan. When there weren't fresh figs to eat, we ate the ones that dried on the stem. Like monkeys we peed from the tree tops. We tried to yell like Tarzan and howl like baboons. We had forts in the sky and our secret ways to get up and down. From our fig jungle we could raid the prunes and cot trees.

REBELLIOUS SIGNS

When the apricots were ripe, workers would pick them and place them on drying racks under the trees. The apricots would be halved, and the seeds taken out. They were sprayed with a lye solution to keep the flies off until dry. Mom always warned us to leave the cots, as we called them, on the trays alone, but we couldn't help but pilfer a few of the delicious morsels. When Kit and I arrived back at the house, Mom proclaimed, "You boys have been into the cots, haven't you!" "No, Mom, No." "You get in the bathroom wash your face and take a look in the mirror." We sprang for the bathroom. How could she know with such conviction; the crime took place hours ago? As I washed the dirt and sticky juice from my face, I could see the cracks forming at the corners of my mouth where the lye solution was eating away at my tender skin.

Mom said, "You are both lucky you didn't poison yourselves. I'm not going to tan your hides, but I can't speak for your dad when he gets home."

"Oh God! What do you think dad will do?"

Dad came rolling into the yard. He dropped his lunch box and gave Mom a kiss. Kit and I remained out of sight where we could still hear them talking. We couldn't tell just what was being said until we heard the words, "Talk to the boys".

Dad said, "Come on boys. Let's go for a walk." We followed him out the back door and around toward where the cots were drying under the trees.

"Which racks did you take the fruit from?"

"We took a couple from each rack, so it wouldn't be obvious they were missing," came Kit's reply.

"Well boys, the owner of this property gives you pretty full reign at most anything within reason, but I kind of think he'd be really displeased if he thought you were stealing his cots that his workers put so much effort into preparing. Not to mention the fact that you could poison yourselves eating them too soon. Come on back to the house. You are going to get a licking and the next time the owner comes by you will both apologize."

We followed Dad back to the house into the kitchen where lickings were generally parceled out.

Now Kit could take a licking without much carrying on, so he didn't have much to say when Dad took his belt off. He still didn't cry till the second or third whack.

Me, I started to wail when Kit got his first whack, and I didn't stop till long after my last one. For some reason I thought a good loud cry would slow Dad's hand, but he saw through my game. By my count Kit and I got the same number of whacks, which were less than we had expected.

Several days later the owner pulled into the yard. Dad was at work, and Kit was at school. Mom said I had to go tell the owner what I had done and apologize for it. She dragged me halfway across the yard before I was convinced, but I made the last few steps on my own and drew myself up to look at the owner. I bawled out an apology and admitted eating from the cot trays. The owner exchanged a few words with my Mom; then looked back at me and said, "So, your daddy gave you a spanking. Good! It's a good thing you didn't poison yourself."

AUNT ADEL AND LOVERBOY

She showed up at our place in a model A Ford with a rumble seat. She would give us kids rides around and around the house and the barn. Aunt Adel could drive and owned her own car even though she was mom's younger sister, and mom, as of yet, did not have a license to drive. That summer, when I was almost five, she called me Lover Boy, because it made her happy, and it made me blush. I did not know the reason for her stay that summer for many years. When I was in my teens, it came to light that Aunt Adel had a baby girl out of wedlock. She gave the child up for adoption staying with us during her last months before giving birth. She was a strong woman. My family was there for her when she really had a need.

BALANCE, TRUST, AND KARMA

One hot summer day Kit and I were out in the orchard next to the house. Bob Elgin, a friend of Dad, had given Kit a baseball and a small bat. We didn't have a glove between us at the time, but we made an effort of hitting and fielding and so on. After a time, Kit became bored with the way things were going and suggested something a little different. "Here," he says, "balance this ball on the top of your head." This was some time before I had learned to question the veracity of some of my brother's advice. "Now hold real still, and I will bat the ball off of your head and way out into the field." I was four years old. He is my big brother. You can be so trusting at that age. I concentrated on being very still balancing the ball right in the center of my head.

I saw the world falling away from me. The ground came up, and I was out like a light. I came to in the living room on the couch. There was ice in a cloth on the back of my head. Mom said that I didn't need stitches cause the goose egg was going to come down. I overheard Mom telling the story to Dad that night. Kit came running into the house yelling, "I've killed Kenny! I've killed Kenny!" Mom then ran out and carried me into the house. I had a goose egg on my head for a couple of days.

FEEDING THE SOW

Across the orchard to the south from us lived the Lashley's, Elmer, Violet and their four kids starting with Kerry who was my age. One morning I was over there with Kerry when his mom told him to take the swill out to the sow. Swill is the waste food and trimmings from the previous several meals prepared for the family. It was common at that time for it to be fed to the pigs and chickens. The sow was in her pen attached to the barn. It had been built to hold a bull so was a substantial structure with thick planks horizontally - spaced over poles set in the ground. The sow lay in her hog house in the barn with her brood of newborn piglets all at her teats. The sun came from behind us lighting the pen while the sow and her brood laid mostly in the shade. Rather than dumping the swill into the trough, we decided to climb into the pen and therefore be able to pelt the sow with her own breakfast. Kerry handed the pan of swill to me through the gap in the planks and climbed in to join me. We started by tossing some bruised tomatoes and half eaten fruit to the sow. She wasn't the least bit interested in our offerings and laid there in all her several hundred pounds of glory enjoying her babies.

It was downright unnatural for that sow to take so little notice of two five-year old's standing in her pig pen. We raised the ante by throwing a couple of raw turnips right at her fat head when all hell broke loose. Piglets were scattering everywhere as the sow raised to her feet. A grunt from her sent them scrambling to the back of the hog house. She turned her attention on me as I gasped amazed at her size. I gauged the distance between us at less than ten feet and saw Kerry climbing for the top of the fence. This was my first real experience with the fight or flight response. The transformation from fat lazy momma pig to feral monster momma pig was instantaneous. Her eyes were like two orange cat's eye marbles intent on ending my existence. Kerry yelled, "Run, Kenny, run." I stepped out and made a lunge for the fence. As I hauled myself up, I could see her coming under my left arm. She got a hold of my pant leg, Blue Bell Wranglers. She tore a piece out of them trousers from cuff to crotch. I hung fast to that fence.

Climbing for the top rail, Momma pig circled the pen a couple of times with my trouser piece hanging out from her mouth. Kerry and I sat there on the top rail looking at each other. How was I going to explain my nearly new wranglers missing a piece up the whole left leg?

That question answered itself when Vi came out of the house. Elmer worked nights at Kaiser Cement, so we were supposed to keep things quiet, so he could sleep. Vi saw me with my left leg and butt cheek hanging out, and the sow with the trouser flag and deduced that we had gone way beyond the chore of feeding the pig.

I could see the look in Vi's eyes much like the one in the momma pigs a few moments before, only with a touch of wild concern like, "Crud! My pig just about ate the neighbor's kid."

She took Kerry and me to the opposite side of the barn, so the noise wouldn't be heard from the house. She said, "Boys, I'm giving you both a spanking. Kenny Boy, you don't know how close you come to getting eaten by a hog." She got herself a twig off a tree in the yard and gave us each a few whacks. Her spanking was a little halfhearted as compared to those metered out by dad, but I put on a good cry to make her feel her efforts weren't in vain, and it helped me to come down from a major adrenaline rush.

Mom patched those pants back together, but one leg was a little narrower than the other.

BIG PURPLE ROCK

In 1953, Kit and I and Kerry were out in the orchard playing cowboys and Indians and gold miners. Kit was the oldest, so he was the cowboy, Kerry was next oldest and the tallest, so he was the Indian, I found a big purple rock that had been turned up when the farmer had disked between the trees. It was about the size of a soft ball. I declared, "It's gold," and carried it around for the rest of the day. We wore shorts and went barefooted out in the orchard all the time. We caught blue belly lizards and horn toads and ate whatever fruit was on the trees. We found ourselves far out in the middle of the orchard when mom called us in to clean up. Walking back across the tilled fields in the afternoon sun I became tired of carrying my big purple rock. I took it in both hands and flung it into the air over my shoulder. I heard a sound like someone's breath being taken away. As I turned around, I saw Kit fall to the ground. His eyes were closed, and he was lifeless. I ran to the house crying and yelling, "Mom, Mom, I've killed Kit." Mom came running out, scooped Kit into her arms and carried him back to the house. He revived a few minutes later, and mom put us both into the bath tub before dad got home. It really was an accident, so neither of us got a licking.

KATHY ENTERS THE SCENE

My baby sister is a year and three months younger than me. Dad called her, Punky, and one thing that Kit and I learned early was that no hair on her head should ever be harmed. By associating with her two brothers though, she did manage to become involved in some of our many capers, which brings me to the time we set one of the sheds on fire.

It was a nice summer day. Kit and I were out of sight from Mom behind a shed on the other side of the driveway from the house. My older brother was instructing me as to the many ways that one could entertain one's self using just a box of household matches. Besides the skill of striking them on the box we were learning to make small projectiles of them. To my recollection this is where the train came off the track. We had stopped several close calls by stomping out the dry grass where errant matches had landed. We were fighting out yet another grass fire when we turned around to find the side of the shed in flames. The flames were above our heads and beyond the point that we could stomp it out. Kit and I ran back across the driveway as the fire leaped up the wall of the shed.

Kathy was playing near the house. We quickly drug her to our hiding place under the porch and gave her the matches. Mom had come flying out of the house at that moment. She pulled out the garden hose and made an effort to fight the fire while telling us to stay where we were. The fire department was on their way. Wow great! I thought now we're going to see something. A big truck came barreling into the drive and three men put out what remained of the shed and the grass. It seemed like the show was over before it even got started. The firemen rolled up their hose and talked to Mom. Then they were gone.

Mom came over by the porch packing a hair brush in her hand. I had never been spanked with a hair brush before, so rather than take a chance I started to cry just as soon as Kit got his first whack. After her firefighting activity and giving my brother a thorough going over you would think that Mom would have been worn out, but she broke that hair brush right over my backside. Then said, "Wait till your dad gets home."

Dad came rolling into the yard at the usual time raising a small cloud of dust in the driveway. Kit and I were laying low hoping for some kind of miracle that would deliver us from the fate we had constructed.

Dad's car was in plain sight of the patch of black grass and burned boards where the shed used to be. We peeped out the window to see Mom talking to dad with Kathy in her arms. Dad stood out starkly in his white painter's overalls against the charred background. Soon enough they started for the house. We ran back to our bedroom hoping to stay out of sight. Kit held up pretty good, but I set up a wail just as soon as I heard Dad's foot on the kitchen floor. I was crying and snorting and blubbering. I had about worn myself out before Dad entered the room. Upon coming in Dad said, "What are you crying about?" I choked, sniffed, and wiped my eyes and then bawled some more. While I continued to warm up, Dad put Kit over his knee and gave him a few whacks. I'm pretty sure I got spanked too. I just remember I didn't stop crying till some time later that evening.

I was a cry baby, but I was a tough little cry baby.

Our family moved from Los Gatos to Santa Clara during Christmas break when I was in kindergarten. The school that would serve our area was not finished yet, so I was shuttled around to three different grammar schools before landing at Bucknell, not far from our house on Comstook Avenue. Our street had twenty-seven houses on each side. It was surrounded by orchards and dead ended into a strawberry field. Nearly every house had at least two kids living in it, so there was a heck of a gang lined up for the school bus most mornings. We were the corner house, so there was a gang of kids lined up in front of our house every school day.

FLIGHT

Dad taught us how to make kites out of sticks and newspaper. We went through a phase where we lost a couple of kites a day to telephone wires or fruit trees. We tried various styles and patterns of kites trying to outdo each other. Dad brought home a kite from the army surplus store. It was about ten feet long and had two control strings made of strong cord. It sat on the shelf in the garage for weeks waiting until dad had time to take us somewhere big and open to fly it. He said it had been used to tow targets behind a ship for gunnery practice. My brother had told all of his friends about the kite so many times they were sick of hearing about it. Somehow the pressure of waiting became too great for him, and he and his friends brought the kite out onto the front yard to unfold it. There were printed instructions for its use and assembly. Before long there on the lawn was the biggest most beautiful kite any of us had ever seen. Where the tail should go there was a rope to tie the target.

A gusty breeze was beginning to puff in from the west. Even on its back the kite seemed to want to fly. Kit and Tom managed to turn the kite over and get the control cords laid out between gusts. Johnny and I held the kite and its tail rope. Kit told Johnny to come take a control rope and he tied the tail rope around my waist freeing my hands to help hold the kite in the ideal flight position. My Big brother knew all about this stuff! Kit lifted the front of the kite off the ground as Tom and Johnny held tension on the cords. Suddenly the kite leapt from my hands into the air followed by the tail rope with me tethered firmly to it. I was jerked off my feet, shot skyward and to my right before you could say Jack Robinson. I slammed to the grass and was about to utter a suggestion concerning safety when I shot up again in the opposite direction. This assent was more remarkable in that I had time to notice the power lines overhead and the looks of both extreme joy and fearful dread on the faces of my brother's friends. As I slammed into the ground a second time, my brother reassured them that we were getting this under control and that a little more practice at the cords would result in smooth flight. My third trip up I was like a rag doll, consigned to my fate of having my legs broken on impact or if the flight was successful being tangled in the telephone wires. At about the point when I reached the high arc on my third flight, I saw Dad's car round the corner. The distraction contributed to a momentary lapse of control by my ground crew, and I once more slammed into the grass. Tom and Johnny were gone by the time I untangled myself from the kite. Dad untied the tail rope from my waist and gave Kit and me a talking to. He said that we weren't to take the kite out anymore without him being there.

THE EL RANCHO DRIVE-IN

About every two weeks the family would load into the car for a trip to the drive-in movie. On this Friday night Dad didn't really want to go, but Mom talked him into it. There was a playground in front of the big screen to keep kids occupied before it became dark enough for the movie to begin. Before the movie there was cartoons and a newsreel. Dad was asleep before the movie even started. After the first movie there was an intermission. It was during this time that the theater would announce the winners of its weekly, monthly and yearly jackpot drawings. We sat there halfheartedly listening to an advertisement for, Reds Hot Tamales, follow the bouncing ball to the snack bar. The weekly winner of the jackpot got fifty dollars and a ham. The monthly winner received three hundred dollars. This happened to be the night that they announced the Yearly winner It would be nine hundred dollars. We heard Dad's name come through the speaker. "Oscar Frederic, come to the snack bar office to claim your prize." Kit and Mom and I and Kathy all started yelling at once. "Dad, Dad wake up you've won the big prize." Dad roused from his slumber to say, "It's probably some kind of scam. I never signed up for no drawing." Mom said, "No, Oscar, I put your name in months ago. Go to the snack bar and claim your prize." After a couple minutes of pleading and cajoling we convinced dad to at least go check it out. He came back after a few minutes to say that they wanted him to stop by such and such a bank the next Friday to pick up his prize. Again, Dad started saying how it was probably a scam and that there wouldn't be any money. Come the next Friday the money was there.

Dad pulled us all together a few nights after the prize money was in the bank and presented us with a question. Would we like a new car or a trip around the United States? We opted for the trip. Our family spent several months of the summer of 1956 traveling by car. We saw the Black Hills, Old Faithful and a host of our country's treasures as we camped and drove all the way to Maine and back. That trip played a big part in forming my idea of who we are as a country.

GLEN GARY ROAD

A cabin in the hills west of Felton became our home when I was seven. It was perched about a quarter of a mile above Highway Nine not far from the edge of the Henry Cowell Redwood State Park. Ours was the last bus stop on the route from San Lorenzo Valley School. From the bus stop at the bottom of the hill it was a steep climb up to our house. Most of the cabins strung along the road were second homes occupied only on weekends when their owners felt like getting away from San Jose or the bay area.

Redwood forest interspaced with tanbark oak, madrone and fir carpeted the valley and canyons leading up from the river. Our school was in double session at the time, so we would not get off the bus till around five in the afternoon. Kit and I would walk up the hill in the dark when the days were short in the winter time. Several times we encountered raccoons raiding the trash cans left near the road by the summer people. We were telling dad about this, and he mentioned there might be a bounty on the raccoons because the fish and game was trying to reduce their populations. We began to hatch a plan to obtain some pelts to make coonskin caps like Davy Crocket on TV. Dad gave us a short length of galvanized pipe filled with sand that would do for a devastating club. Armed with that and a flashlight, we laid out our plan. We stashed the club and light in the bushes near the bus stop to be handy for our walk up the hill for home. Kit and I were full of anticipation as we gathered our gear and began our quiet stalk up the hill. The first several cans were unmolested as we made our way up the dark forested road. As we came near to the third set of cans, we could hear scratching and kind of a happy growling sound emanating from a heavy GI can with the lid removed. I turned my flashlight on the opening to the can as Kit advanced from the side where he would have a clear swing without blocking the light. Just as Kit got into position, the raccoon stuck his head up above the rim of the can. My brother swung that iron club down on the head of that raccoon like Babe Ruth knocking in a home run. The can made a heck of a racket when the pipe came in contact with it, but the raccoon lay quiet as a stone. Kit reached in to retrieve our trophy. He had it about half way out when it sprang back to life. Using Kit's arm like a cat climbs a tree, that coon clawed his way up out of the can and over the top of Kit's head leaving claw marks and scratches about every square inch of the way. I last saw a flash of him when he bounded from the top of Kit's head to a nearby tree.

My flashlight was losing its battery strength and wasn't much help in inspecting Kits wounds. It didn't matter much. We knew the road and the trails well enough to make our way home without it. On the way I heard a whole bunch of new words I had never imagined were in my brother's lexicon, and it didn't stop when we retold our version of the event to Pop. Mom brought out the hydrogen peroxide and iodine, so when we sat down for dinner, Kit looked like he'd been in a fight with a cheese grater.

That homemade pipe club was around the place for several years after that, but it never again saw the use for which it was intended.

Living in the redwoods and having access to Henry Cowell Park was wonderful. Mom worked at the concession stand with the head ranger's wife selling burgers and sodas to park visitors in the summer time. We kids roamed the forest and river always on a new adventure.

Dad and Mom loved to barbeque and have friends and family over to the place. They would play cards till late into the night while we ran through the woods playing hide and go seek or tag. We had a place below the cabin where trees grew together over a gully in a small canyon. Kit and I had hung ropes from the branches in such a way that you could swing from tree to tree. With two or more kids we could swing for hours without ever touching ground.

We lived there out of Felton for five years until I was in the seventh grade.

SCOTTS VALLEY

During Christmas break we moved to our new home built on eight acres on Vine Hill Road. It was a transition for all of us leaving the redwoods for more open grass lands with permanent neighbors close by. The first local boy I met was the kid across the street. It was a cloudy day with a light breeze and a spit of rain. I saw him on his side of the road and pretended not to notice him, acting as though I was looking at something on the ground. A grass bomb landed a few inches from my feet. I picked it up and threw it at the kid. We began plucking up more grass and heaving it back and forth making a muddy mess of each other and the street between. One of the kid's older brothers came out to watch the contest and two more much older brothers joined him. When I would bend down to pick up more ammunition, I would rise to see that the brothers were resupplying the Kid. With their help he was able to maintain a steady volume of in-coming while I had to spend time gathering ammo. After a few minutes I was covered with mud and standing in a pool of muddy grass bombs. The kid was looking pretty good compared to me when the oldest brother said, "I think the little bugger is alright!" That is how I met the Roesner Boys:

Ronny, Richard, Robby and the youngest Roger who was to become my closest friend. Roger and I made bows and arrows and learned to shoot them well enough to be a threat to most small game and birds within walking distance of home.

SKUNKS

There was a chicken ranch up the road from us. Diego, the owner would pay us 25 cents for every rat and 50 cents for every skunk we would kill and bring to him. One evening in the fall, Steve and Ted Cox, along with Roger and I, set out to reduce the skunk population in and around Diego's chicken ranch. We each had a bow and eight to ten arrows. We used our worst arrows on skunks, mostly 25 cent target arrows. We set up on a little rise overlooking the ranch where we could see the tails of the skunks as they made their way across the fields headed for the chicken barns. In the fall the skunks would still be in family units with one or two adults and three to seven mostly grown younger ones. When we would spot a bunch of them, we would surround them and start shooting them full of arrows. When we had dispatched one bunch, we would pick them up touching only our arrows and deposit them into a gunny sack. We hooped and yelled like wild Indians and found another bunch, then another until we had two sacks with twenty skunks in them. We had lost a lot of arrows in the grass and were down to just two or three apiece. Roger spotted a big boar skunk, and we were off to nail him. We fired all our arrows, and he was still able to make headway through the grass with four of our arrows sticking out of him. Roger came up with an old dish pan that was laying in the field and managed to place it over the fleeing skunk. By placing one foot on the dish pan Roger was able to hold the skunk down while not getting sprayed and extricate our arrows. He handed us each one arrow, and we surrounded the dish pan. We stepped back a couple of feet and waited for the skunk to bolt. Moments went by with no movement or sound coming from the pan. Roger used the end of his bow to flip the pan off the skunk. As the big ole boar raised up to spray, Roger kicked him. That skunk went skyward in a spinning ark spraying all four of us in the process. Upon returning to earth we put four arrows into him pinning him to the ground. We bagged him and transported our skunks over to Diego's back door in the trunk of Steve's car. Diego was very pleased that we had killed twenty-one skunks in one night, and we were happy to relieve him of ten dollars and fifty cents.

All of us had missed dinner and there wasn't much chance of us getting any at home, smelling like we did. We decided to head over to Snow White Drive In for a burger. As we approached the drive in, from the car a wall of stink went before us causing the patrons inside to immediately head for the exits. The girls behind the counter backed as far away from us as possible while taking our orders then asked us to wait outside. Our orders would be brought out to us. As we waited, a few customers tried to reenter the restaurant, but the smell was so pervasive that their attempts were in vain. A few young male customers wanted to make trouble, but they couldn't get close enough to us to make good on their threats.

After ridding the town of twenty-one skunks in one night we were out cast by our fellow citizens. We received a welcome at home not unlike that at Snow White. None of us slept in the house that night. Roger and I took baths in vinegar and dish soap and buried our clothes in the back yard for a few days.

There is no doubt in my mind that it was the greatest single skunk hunt in Scotts Valley history.

1960 SANTA CRUZ

Living in Santa Cruz County in the sixties was like being Alice in Wonderland. The Beat Nik culture morphed into the Hippie culture and began to be an influence as I entered my teens. A group of people from the bay area took over the old barn that sat at the end of Granite Creek Road. It was an old dairy barn before being used as the fire station. Then some Stanford University guy got it to conduct experiments. From our house we could hear the loud music that emanated from the barn on Friday and Saturday nights. Roger and I made several attempts to get in and listen to the bands that would come to play. The guys running it would let us hang out during the day but would run us off about the time the band showed up. Roger's mother had gone to a costume party with her boyfriend dressed as two of the Beatles. We found the wigs they had worn and reasoned that if we had long hair the Hippies would let us hang out and listen to the music. We arrived at the barn around four in the afternoon, it was late fall, but still warm out. Roger and I had our standard uniforms on: Levis, white T-shirts and Converse tennis shoes.

With the Beatle wigs we looked like a couple of twin Beatle miniatures. We mixed with the people setting up for the evening's event for a few minutes then hid on the lower level where we could watch what was going on unseen. At about five thirty they began to usher everyone out except for the band and those putting on the event. We stayed hidden, this was the time that in the past they had always asked us to leave. After a few minutes two people brought a stainless-steel coffee urn and sat it up on a counter in the kitchen area. Next to the urn they placed a stack of small paper cups, the kind with the folds in them like you used to see at water bottles in offices. Roger and I remained hidden wanting to learn more about what was going on. Twenty or more people filed into the room and formed a line leading to the coffee urn. One by one they were each given a cup of liquid which they drank as they exited the room. Soon Roger and I were the only ones left in the room. We emerged from our hiding spot and went directly to the urn. We each filled a cup with purple liquid and tasted it. Kool Aid, it was just Kool Aid! Why would anyone make such a big deal about Kool Aid? We made our way back to our hiding spot to talk it over. We had expected white lightning or vodka but just plain old Kool Aid? After a few minutes we decided to go upstairs to the dance floor. Emerging from the left side of the stage on the dance floor we took in all the commotion as the band was setting up. This very flamboyant woman sat on the edge of the stage facing us with a bottle of whiskey in one hand as she talked loudly to the band.

She was captivating to my fifteen-year-old mind. Very much in charge of the room in a purple paisley satin dress with a stole that sat on her shoulders and accentuated her every movement. We stood before her transfixed like a couple of waifs looking through a candy store window at the treats they could never afford. Something about us caught her attention, and she looked our way. She said, "Come here, boys!" Somehow, we crossed the several steps into her open and upraised arms. She hugged us tightly and embraced us with our faces tucked snugly in her breasts. In that moment I drank in the smell of the whiskey, the perfume, and the smoke. She released us, and we stepped back in a state of transfixion. A guy asked us if we wanted to help him with the light show. We said OK and moved up to an elevated area near the back of the dance floor. There was an overhead projector set up with some clear glass dishes that we would pass under the light that would project them on to the wall behind the band. The dishes had various colored oils and liquids that bubbled and flowed with the sounds coming from the band.

The dance floor filled with people as the strobe light blinked in cadence. An announcer stepped forward to introduce Big Brother and The Holding Company and to welcome the Mary Pranksters.

I don't remember the band ever taking a break until after midnight when the announcer said, "The Prankster bus is leaving for La Honda." Roger and I looked at each other and thought, "Ever been to La Honda?" We thought better of it and decided to head for home. Outside in the fresh night air our heads began to clear, just a little. We could either walk home over the overpass and along the road or up the creek that flowed through a tunnel under the freeway. We opted for the creek. We were less than a half mile from home.

We reached the entrance to the tunnel with no trouble. The tunnel ran for several hundred feet under the freeway and had a bend in the middle preventing us from seeing end to end. I told Roger that I was seeing all sorts of things that I didn't ordinarily see. He said that the same thing was happening to him. We concluded that this must be what you feel like when you listen to loud music and see strobe lights.

The tunnel under the freeway was made of cement about eight feet wide by ten feet tall. There was always a large population of daddy long legs spiders hanging from its ceiling and the top of the wall. At the entrance there was a little ambient light where we paused to gaze into the black mouth of the tunnel before us. I says to Roger, "I'm seeing piles and piles of huge monster spiders." He says to me, "Man I'm having the same dream." We made it to the other end of the tunnel with little trouble and emerged into the creek bed on the other end. It took us all night to transverse the few blocks to home. We kept seeing faces in the roots of the trees that lined the creek bed. At that time in our lives neither one of us had ever taken any drugs. Our explanation for feeling the way we did was rock and roll music, strobe lights and having the same dream.

Over time I learned that the woman who hugged us that night was Janis Joplin, and the band was Big Brother and the Holding Company, and that the Kool Aid we drank had LSD in it. I didn't go to sleep that next day until late in the night.

THE DRAFT

My draft notice reached me in June, stating that my fellow citizens had chosen me to serve our country and that I would be inducted on the 29th of July 1969.The last weeks of civilian freedom flew by. I quit working for George, sold my motorcycle and spent my remaining time visiting with family and friends. I went to one party at the home of one of the guys I rode dirt bikes with. At some time late in the evening, my friend Steve Wallace, stood me up on a chair and pronounced to the crowd, "Kenny's headed for Vietnam." There was a short round of whooping and yelling, and as things grew quiet, a voice from the back of the room said, "Kill a couple of gooks for me." The statement put only a momentary damper on the party, but it stuck in my head. That was the expectation… that I was chosen to go and to kill. My draft notice said that I would enter the service on July 29th, 1969. Prior to receiving my induction notice, I figured that the war would be over before I went in. President Nixon had been re-elected saying he would end the war in Vietnam.

I couldn't evade the draft as some of the guys I knew were doing. My family history didn't allow it! My Dad had been at Iwo Jima driving marines ashore in the landing boats. He saw with his own eyes the flag rising on Mount Suribachi. Aunt Joyce served as a WAC. Uncle Eddy was nearly killed losing an arm and a bunch of intestines when the ship he was on was struck by a kamikaze at the battle for Okinawa. Uncle Bob was a conscientious objector yet still he drove ambulance for Patton's Army from Normandy till the liberation of the death camp at Bocanval. Uncle Louie also served in the army through Europe and was involved in the Battle of The Bulge. Both of my grandfathers served in the army during the First World War.

 Coming from this background, there was no way I was going to refuse to serve. I sold my truck and my motorcycle and proceeded to party till my date of induction.

 My older brother and my cousin had joined the Air Force over the past couple of years to serve without having to fight on the ground in Vietnam. My thinking was that President Nixon had been elected on a promise to end the war. I wasn't of a mind set to give up four years to serve in the other branches of the armed forces. I was not very good with authority. I reasoned that two tough years would go by quicker, and besides, it would most likely be over before I got there.

 Time was to teach me about just how wrong my suppositions were. I put on a brave face and said goodbye to family and friends. My girlfriend saw me off at the bus station with a declaration of love and faithfulness and a lingering kiss that made me want to believe that I would be back soon.

The bus pulled out of Santa Cruz and up over Hwy 17. As the redwoods and the view of Monterey Bay dropped behind, I felt the pull of memories-the wonderful family I have been blessed to be a part and of the great community of friends from Felton, Ben Lomond, Scotts Valley, Soquel, Aptos, Capitola and Santa Cruz.

BASIC TRAINING

Then there was an airliner, and then the bus to Fort Lewis. We arrived in the afternoon, so there wasn't enough time to begin processing us. We were run through a chow line and given a bunk for the night. In the minutes before lights out, the talk went to Vietnam and how many of us would be going over. I remember thinking that just nine days ago I was watching a guy walk on the moon at the Detrick's house. Now I've been drafted into our nation's army to serve.

We came awake to the yelling of a couple of hold overs (guys who didn't have an assignment after basic for some reason).

They got us up and out and on the way to chow by six in the morning. Waiting for us, as we came out of the mess hall, was the man who would do the most to transform us from being civilians.

His name was Drill Sgt. Page, five foot ten, back as straight as a hoe handle, made of black-brown leather. He wore his faded olive drab utilities starched. His campaign hat sat firmly on his head at just enough angle to notice. His total demeanor was of a man in control of the situation. He seldom had to yell at us. In a voice just a little above conversation he could get a platoon of draftees to fall in and dress right. He did most of it with his eyes. When he looked at you, you could see the war he'd been through and sense that he would prepare you to go there, too.

We were off to get our hair cut. Four barbers went through 48 of us in less than an hour. A couple of black guys with big afros, saw their hair on the floor in one piece. A basketball size bundle of tight curls; pride being stripped away. We all felt it.

By the end of the day we all wore the same uniforms, had the same number of the same color socks and could be moved from place to place by a column of twos. I thought it couldn't get worse, but then I was told, I would have KP in the morning.

The fire watch woke me at four, and I made my way through the fog over to the mess hall to report in to the mess sergeant. I was put to work in a cold area of the kitchen operating a potato peeling machine. After an hour of operating the machine, I was wet and cold. The mess sergeant said I could get a cup of coffee. It was the only hot liquid available. Although I'd never enjoyed coffee at that point in my life, a change took place. I'll always remember that cup of coffee and the mess sergeant's simple invitation.

At 0600 I was back with my platoon. We fell in to have SSG Page teach us the exercises of Army Drill 1. Our platoon was all U.S., that is drafted. The other three platoons making up CO E-32 were mostly volunteers. As a result, we were low platoon on the pecking order. We took a little more crap from the cadre just to let us know that a volunteer RA troop was worth a little more than a draftee.

In those first weeks the other platoons could outrun us and had faster times through the obstacle course. Most of us had been out of high school for a couple of years. We had a couple of 25-year olds. We called them the old men.

During the first day of basic, we were broken up into 12-man squads. My squad chose Jim, a Korean kid from San Jose, to be our squad leader, and I was chosen as his assistant squad leader. As it turned out Jim broke a leg about a week into training, and I became squad leader.

I was a fighter homegrown. My older brother by two years (Kit) lived to tease. When we would get to going at it, Dad would put boxing gloves on us and give my brother the opportunity to do a little sparring. Kit was head and shoulders taller than me, so I got a lot of practice boxing, wrestling and street fighting a larger opponent.

I was the shortest kid at Soquel High School. When a freshmen or sophomore wanted to test themselves on a senior, they would come looking for the little guy with the chip on his shoulder. I had my share of quick one rounders and a few knockdown drag outs. When I graduated, I was just over five feet tall.

To understand where I was headed you need to really see where I had come from. I've got to mention my single most important Influence at this point in my life. He was my neighbor and best friend from 7th grade through high school. His name is Roger, and he had three older brothers Ronnie, Richard and Robbie. Roger's mom was single and cared for her four boys by running a nursing home out of her house. The boys slept and did most of their living out in the garage. The yard was full of activity day and night with hotrods and motor bikes. The boys always kept a couple of big dogs and a coop full of pigeons. Roger and I spent our days and nights with bows and arrows, sling shots, BB guns, 22's and fishing poles. We moved through the woods and creeks and back yards of Scotts Valley for six years, often at night. Little did I know how well those experiences were to serve me.

Basic Training went on in a rainstorm of hurry up and wait. Drill Sergeant Page and the cadre drilled us with the M14. We marched and ran and double-timed everywhere we went. We slept with the windows open at night to prevent some disease from spreading through the ranks. One morning after chow we were told to take our mattresses to the laundry to be deloused. We accomplished this one man in front and one in back with a mattress under each arm.   Myself and my partner were making our way in front of the next barracks past a troop who was raking the dirt in front of the barracks next to ours.

 I stepped off of the side walk in order to give the guys coming back with their clean mattresses room to pass us. The trooper doing the raking dropped his rake and swung a loose right hook at the side of my head. Dropping the mattress, I threw a couple of quick punches and went for a take-down against the side of the barracks. My taller opponent wasn't ready for me to be on top of him. I managed to land a little strike to his wind pipe and he was all mine. A crowd formed around us and just as I was able to press my advantage, Drill Sergeant Page pulled me off him. He stood me at attention and said, "Frederic, you little banty rooster! What are you doing, starting a fight with that first platoon troop?" Several guys who saw the trooper swing on me first, spoke up, saying, "Frederic didn't start it Drill Sergeant. He did!" SSG Page brought that trooper to attention and got eyeball to eyeball and says, "Why did you swing on Frederic?" "That trooper stepped in my dirt." SSG Page bent forward and reaching to the ground brought a pinch of dirt to his nose, locked eyeball to eyeball with him and said, "This smells like US Army dirt to me." At that moment the tension dropped ninety percent, and we went about changing our mattresses out.

Later that day in the barracks, SSG Page gave us a talk about if we were going to fight someone it should not be someone from our own platoon. He was able to take that incident and weave it into his plan to form us into a unit. He called us his "Misfits". Within a few weeks we were matching and beating the other platoons at close order drill and the other skills that make a soldier.

There were some guys in our platoon that didn't need to be there. The selective service cast a pretty wide net. Over the first month of basic most of these guys were transferred to the hold over platoon, where they would eventually be processed out of the army. We had one guy, Hippy Tom, who swallowed a bunch of sleeping pills. I had fire watch that night and found the empty pill bottle on the floor next to his bunk. SSG Page got him up and sent to the mess hall for burnt toast and coffee. Hippy Tom threw up, got his stomach pumped and joined us for training late the next morning. A few days after that we were training on armored personnel carriers. We were riding on top hanging onto large D rings. It was a cold foggy morning, one of those wet fogs like you're moving through a rain cloud. We were moving along a tank road over rock and big gravel. Between the noise of the engines and the crash, crunch, and screech of the tracks you couldn't hear yourself scream. As the treads came round the wheels, they tended to give the vehicle a looping motion, back and forth. Most of my attention was taken up by just holding on and trying to stay warm. From my position near the front of the track I was facing backward, Hippy Tom was at the back. Fixing his gaze on me I saw a look in his eyes, like something strange was about to take place. Tom launched himself backwards like a diver doing a backward flip off of the track, directly into the path of the track behind. Only the quick reaction on the track driver saved Tom's life. He threw his track to his left stopping so as to partially block the road in front where Tom lay. Our end of the column came to a stop several hundred yards up in the fog.   I saw Tom once more several weeks after that incident. The Army had made him a Chaplain's Assistant.

Basic Training has several required courses each trainee must fulfill in order to pass through to the next stage of his training. One of these is the Fire and Movement course. I had to pull KP on the day that our company did the fire and movement course, so I had to make it up by completing the course with another company. Several of us were transported out to the range in a company jeep to join the other company. I spent the morning and part of the afternoon setting on bleachers in the rain watching the other trainees go through the exercise. It was live fire with the M14 rifle. Trainees six at a time were to advance up a small hill. Each one of them had a sergeant behind them keeping score and guiding them through the process. At the bottom of the hill each trooper had a full magazine. As he went up the hill, various targets would present themselves. The trooper was expected to engage each target then move on to the next one. At the top of the hill the trooper's weapon was cleared, and he was scored on his performance. From here he would exit into a ditch about ten feet deep and twenty feet wide, moving out of the ditch at the far end around the hill and back to the bleachers. Several of the guys who had completed the course had told me that when you get finished with the course get the hell out of that ditch as soon as possible. The sergeants who scored the course rode out of the ditch in a one-ton weapons carrier and were making a game out of splashing as much mud as possible on the trainees as they exited the ditch. My turn at the course finally came. A sergeant was assigned to me, and we began our assault at the hill. After watching the other trainees all day, I had a pretty good idea of how to take on the targets while staying on line. When we reached the top of the hill, I removed the clip from my weapon, but before I opened the bolt to clear it, the sergeants clearing me and scoring me both headed for the weapons carrier. I slung my M14 over my shoulder and ran for the exit, out of the ditch. I put on a burst of speed but could hear the weapons carrier coming along throwing mud as it came. I could also hear one of the sergeants yelling, "Come to port arms, come to port arms!" through a bull horn. Jumping out of the ditch and onto the grass, I slowed my pace and came to port arms. Just then, I was able to separate all the noise and my effort from having double timed out of the ditch. I was about to catch my breath when a black drill sergeant I had never seen before stepped out of the passing weapons carrier and began to instruct me in the difference between sling and port arms. He was carrying a range flag wrapped around a piece of inch and one-half closet rod about thirty inches long. As he berated me, he struck at me with the closet rod. On the second or third hit I tried to turn away from the blow taking it on my neck at the base of my skull just under my helmet. I went out like a light. As I came to, there was a guy standing over me saying, "I wouldn't take that from nobody." I was at present in a frame of mind to agree with him and pointed my M14 in the general direction of the drill sergeant who was walking away. I squeezed off the round that was still in the chamber. It was as though the whole world went silent for a moment. From my position, flat on my back, it seemed everyone at the range was looking at me. The drill sergeant regained his composure and came charging at me. With my bayonet still fixed to the end of my weapon as part of the course, I assumed a defensive position. Somehow, he sensed that I wasn't going to let him get behind me again. When he said that he was going to march me down to the range shack, I said, "No, I'll march you down to the range shack." Off we went to the range shack. When we reached that location, all the sergeants and officers for the company were there. I surrendered my weapon to a lieutenant at the door and was ushered inside. There I was berated by everyone from the sergeant major to the captain and a few lieutenants for good measure. Tears were leaking from my eyes as I was told I could get life in prison. When they were finished dressing me down, I was escorted outside and told to stand at attention until further notice. As I was waiting there trying to get my emotions under control, a black drill sergeant came up to me and asked, "Are you the trainee who was involved in the incident when the shot was fired?" "Yes, drill sergeant," I replied. "Come with me," he ordered. I followed the drill sergeant over behind some freight cars that had been placed there to store materials to keep the range functioning. When we reached a car near the end, the sergeant stopped near a fir tree and told me to remove my helmet and field jacket. I dropped my steel pot to the ground and was beginning to remove the field jacket when he threw his first punch. I dodged around trying to ward off his attack while untangling from the jacket. Once free of the coat I began to give him some of what he was giving me. I managed to back him up to the train car where he went down. By holding onto the car, I was able to heel stomp him several times in the ribs and was working my way up to his head. At that point my brain kicked in and said now would be the appropriate time to stop before I made even more trouble for myself. Gathering up my field jacket and helmet, I returned to where I had been standing at attention. From my post I watched the drill sergeant return to his platoon and begin talking to them as he walked among them.

I could not hear what was being said, but I suspected it had to do with me; they would look my way as they were talking. The drill sergeant and one of his trainees were headed my way. As they came near, I could see that he had chosen his biggest black trainee to bring along. He stopped the trainee at two paces in front of me and asked him if he would like to kick this white boy's ass. The trainee said, "No, drill sergeant, I won't". As I looked that big man in the eyes, a moment of understanding flowed between us. My day was long from over.

The drill sergeant moved away toward his platoon, and I lost track of him for the time being. He was to speak to me just one more time to tell me that he was going to make it his personal business to make sure I went to Vietnam and got the worst shit hole assignment when I got there.

Back at attention, I was hoping this day would pass when a lieutenant approached me. He put me at ease and spoke kindly toward me for a few minutes before coming to his point. He had been present all through the day and was part of an investigation into violations within this company in the way it metered out justice to its trainees. He said that if a man is rendered unconscious, he could not be held accountable for his actions for the several seconds after he regained consciousness. He had been in the bleachers and had seen me struck by the drill sergeant earlier in the day. He warned me against bringing him up to this company but said that he would be in contact with my CO and not to worry. He left me there at attention until a jeep arrived from my own company to pick me up.

I retrieved my weapon from the range shack and climbed into the jeep driven by our company clerk. His first words to me were, "Man, you really threw the shit into the fan! You are in for an ass chewing from the first sergeant, and I don't know what else. You could be looking at stockade time." My nerves were shot from the fire and movement course, the shot at the DI, getting dressed down by the brass, the fight with the second DI and now I have to go before the First Sergeant and the CO and get reamed out again. Is this nightmare ever going to stop?

We arrived back at the company area where I presented myself to the First Sergeant. He kept me waiting for some time to get in to see the Captain. After maybe an hour the First Sergeant told me to report back to my platoon to resume my regular training schedule.

Three times after that, I was called in to see the CO. All three times the first sergeant sent me back to the platoon after not seeing the CO. On that third occasion the First Sergeant confided in me that the company I had gone through the fire and movement course with was under some sort of internal investigation and that I would be best served to forget the incident and go on about my training. I never heard another word about the incident from the army.

Growing up as I had around Santa Cruz, I wasn't exposed to a lot of racial problems. My family did not use racially derogatory language. However, I had heard it outside of the home. None of it prepared me for what was passing as the norm within the ranks at that time. Cussing of all kinds and demeaning phrases were woven in to everyday language by the cadre, by the instructors (most of whom were Vietnam vets) and as time went on by us. One that we heard many times a day was, "California, the land of steers and queers, which one are you?" This was a mild poke used by many of the non-Californians to let us know just how inferior they thought we were.

I only bring this up at this time to let the reader know that we existed at that time in a linguistic cesspool. None the less, it served to separate us from the life we were leaving behind and give us a glimpse of where we were headed. It is my intention not to revert to a lot of foul language in the telling of this. Please remember, we were a lot of young men preparing to go to war. We tried to strike a bad ass pose to cover the reluctance that was a part of each of us. The hippies protested on the TV. The black men seethed and fought for their rights. Women joined in the chorus for equality and sexual liberation, and we prepared for a war in a little country that has since ceased to exist. Our country had just put a man on the moon, and John Kennedy's words, "Ask not what your country can do for you, but what you can do for your country", still resonated. To say we were a confused lot is to put it mildly, but we had been called to serve and like men before us we stepped forward.

Transforming young men into soldiers is a brutal process. Our latrine had nine toilets laid out in a U-shaped pattern with no dividers. We ate, slept, studied and exercised at the same time. So, it stands to reason that we used the latrines at the same time. Anyone with a reluctance to do his thing in front of others was soon cured of that hang up. We bonded at a level few people outside of that experience can know. I can only remember the names of a couple of guys I went through basic with, but I still remember their faces and how we helped each other through that time.

We received our orders for our MOS (military occupational specialty) near the end of our training. I had decided to extend my enlistment and go, Airborne Ranger Green Beret. I was headed for the Infantry, and I figured I ought to be as prepared as possible. Upon hearing this, Drill Sergeant Page took me aside and said, "Frederic, I've been in this man's army for seventeen years. Do your two years and get out." I heeded his advice.

Over half of our platoon were assigned to the infantry and sent to other training bases. My new post was about a half mile walk across the parade field. As I made that march, alone, with my duffel bag, I wondered. Did that DI from the other company make good on his threat by keeping me here at Fort Lewis?

ADVANCED INFANTRY TRAINING

My new platoon sergeant was a "Shake and Bake," a regular trainee given extra training to fill buck sergeant slots because of the rate of attrition in the war. I was the first trainee to show up for this training cycle. After introducing himself as Sergeant Blake, he made me acting squad leader of first squad. Over the next two days another forty-seven guys showed up to fill out the platoon.

Sergeant Blake was about five eleven with a paunch that he had learned to live with. He had almost black hair that was a little longer than regulation and always a five-o-clock shadow. He liked to sneak around the company area looking for a reason to make a trainee do pushups or rifle PT. His example caused me to believe that all shake and bakes were substandard. Later, I would learn this was not so. Blake did not instill confidence in those around him although he was just one buck sergeant in the company.

Lucius Parr was made second squad leader. He was from Alabama, and we became instant friends. He grew up in the church singing gospel songs, and he could belt out the sweetest cadence on the North Fort. He and I had some good talks about faith and family where I got some first looks into his world, and he into mine. He said that I was his first white friend.

Private Vacianary was from Texas. He was a golden gloves boxer, spoke extremely broken English, had a bad attitude all the time and was in my squad. When one of us in the squad made a mistake, we all had to do pushups or rifle PT, most often because of Pvt. Vacianary. After four days of extra pushups and several sessions of rifle PT in the rain, we were all fed up with his attitude. It fell on me to communicate to him that a change was necessary. He knew what was coming when I shook him awake on his top bunk. He came off the bunk swinging and connecting almost at will. I was able to get in close and bring him to the floor before the rest of my squad jumped in and prevented him from really beating the crap out of me. I had a nice bruise and a cut lip but considered myself lucky given the skill, speed and power that Vacianary had unleashed on me.

I was called into the First Sergeant's office to make a report and to discuss what punishment would be metered out to Vacianary. I requested that he receive no punishment, and that he be reassigned to another unit. The first sergeant asked if I would like a little one on one with him to get even. I nixed that idea, thinking, "Hell No!" The last thing I wanted was another opportunity for that buzz saw to get at me. In my mind, he was just a guy from Mexico who got caught up in the draft and was pissed off at the world. I figured it would take more than what I could give or understand to turn him toward what the army wanted.

Jesse was another story. He was from West Virginia and called me squad leader - always squad leader. He said he had never driven on a paved road until he reported for the draft. He had no teeth because the army had pulled them all, and he was waiting for the swelling to go down so that false ones could be made. He would eat anything that came through the mess hall and swore it was the best he ever had. We helped him study for his GED whenever there was time, sometimes in the latrine after lights out. He eventually got his GED and new teeth before the end of our training cycle. Later, in Vietnam, I saw Jesse at the Bob

Hope show in Vietnam. He had been field commissioned as a Lieutenant. I always knew he was one of the smartest guys I had ever met, but with his West Virginia upbringing, we didn't know it.

Billy was from Georgia. He wasn't in my squad, but third squad upstairs. He had been to jump school and was the only one in our platoon who had. He had an "I don't give a damn attitude" that drew me to him at first. I was up in his squad bay, about a week into AIT when a fight broke out down on the ground between the barracks buildings. The fight was between Lucius and a white guy I didn't recognize. We had a good view of the whole thing. Lucius was holding his own pretty well when Billy yells out the window, "Kick that nigger's ass." I turned on Billy and said, "Hey man, that's Lucius down there." Billy said he didn't care and that I was a chump to be calling any black man my friend. That ended any friendly relations between me and Billy. By the time I got downstairs the fight was over. Neither of them was hurt. It was just some minor grudge that was over when the last punch was thrown. No officers or noncoms saw it, and nobody ratted. Things didn't work out so simple between Billy and me. Several days later it was my squad's turn to serve in the chow line. Each squad took turns at serving breakfast. I was at the end of the line handing each man that wanted one an orange. Billy's squad was moving through the line. When he got to me, he gave me a dirty look, and I put an orange on his tray. He helped himself to another orange out of the box in front of me which I quickly took back explaining to him that there wasn't enough to go around, so he could only have one. He said he was going to get my nigger loving ass. Over the next several days tension was high between him and me and our respective squads.

This morning the mess hall was serving chipped beef on toast, known as, shit on a shingle. It turned out that Billy's squad was serving that morning, and Billy was standing behind the sneeze guard serving the toast. When I reached his station, he refused to serve me, and when I reached under the sneeze guard to get some, Billy struck me on the hand with the serving tongs. I moved on a little farther towards the chipped beef then faked as though reaching back for a piece of toast. When Billy swung at my left hand, I was ready with my right and grabbed him at the collar of his utility shirt. Pulling Billy head first into the serving tray of chipped beef I was able to administer several short lefts to his head while our two squads broke into a general melee over the steam table. The whole thing was over as quick as it began. Each side blamed the other for starting it, and we got our chow and headed out to the day's training. We were there to learn to fight and to go to war, and I guess the brass didn't much split hairs about a small scuffle in the mess hall.

We learned about fragmentation grenades and booby traps. We went daily to the ranges to be instructed on the fifty-caliber machine gun or the forty-five-caliber pistol or the M-79 grenade launcher. We became familiar with the M-60 machine gun, and we lived with and went everywhere with our M-16s. We were instructed in first aid and CPR and what to do for a sucking chest wound. All the while Sergeant Blake was sneaking around trying to catch one of us far enough from our M-16 for him to grab it, so he could punish us with more pushups or rifle PT.

REAL TRAINING

The ranges were manned almost exclusively by infantry vets who returned from Vietnam. Those guys went out of their way in an effort to pass on the vital information about staying alive. They schooled us on squad tactics and tried to get across to us the importance of being able to keep your head and be quiet in the bush. We were trained in hand to hand combat and the use of the bayonet. We trained with fixed bayonet on our M-16s on dummies or in formation learning to parry right or left or butt stroke. After several weeks of this we advanced to pugil training. For this exercise two combatants face each other in a ring. Each has a mock rifle with padding at the two ends and a face guard like a catcher's mask that fits on with a helmet over. A referee calls for the match to begin, and the two begin to exercise the skills taught in bayonet training. If one opponent is successful several times, he is matched with a larger opponent or even two opponents to further test his skills. At no time is it legal within the rules to turn the pugil around and use it like a baseball bat nor could you strike a man on the ground.

We had all had a turn at pugil training and were having a second go at it. I was matched with a larger opponent for my second bout and was able to turn him aside with a parry left and a butt stroke to the head. Up to this point it was all affable. No one was out to do harm to his opponent. It was decided I would go against two. Who should step up to oppose me but Billy. He was joined by another guy in his squad. I didn't know the other guy, so I figured he didn't have a bone to pick with me. My strategy was to put Billy on the ground first, because I knew he wanted to see me hurt badly, and then I would go for the second guy if he hadn't already laid me out.

The referee placed us at our starting places. The platoon was all around us. Over the past weeks Billy's squad had lost enthusiasm for his hatred for me which had become an outlet of his hatred for blacks. This was between Billy and me. It was a fight I did not want. Here he came. In his hurry he stepped ahead of his teammate making it easier to engage him as an individual. He was on my right, so by stepping far to my right I was able to put Billy between me and his partner. There was a flurry of strokes, and I was able to put Billy on the ground. Now the bout was between me and the second. We were hard at it when I could hear a yell from my squad. The second delivered a legal thrust that drove me back; Billy landed a roundhouse swing that put me down. As I lay there on my back, I saw Billy through my face guard. He stood over me and brought that pugil down like a sledge hammer on a spike.

I came to in Madigan Hospital. Who was in the bed next to me but Billy! I had broken two teeth off that would have to be extracted and had a fat lip. I'm not sure how extensive Billy's injuries were but I guess the guys in my squad worked him over pretty well. He didn't make it out to training with us the next day. He was held over to finish training with another company. I was to see Billy one more time in Vietnam. I'll say more on that later.

When I rejoined my squad, it was late in the day. Lucius and Jesse and the others told me how they had yelled a warning when Billy came after me the second time. They had rushed forward to stop him but were unable to get there before he brought the hammer down. In the crush that followed liberties were taken; Billy would no longer train with us.

SIMULATED JUNGLE TRAINING

It was November in Washington out at the RTA (Rainer Training Area). We were given one sleeping bag for every two men. There was anywhere from two inches to a foot of snow in the rain forest where our jungle training was to take place. In the daytime we practiced fire and movement and clearing villages. I managed to trip a booby trap and blow myself up in all three of the villages I was supposed to help clear. The one night we spent out there

110

was a wet cold mess. We dug fox holes in the mud and fended off an aggressor force and infiltrators all night. The range NCO's earnestly tried to school us on clearing mines and sweeping a village. But in the snow and the slush and so close to being at the end of our training, everyone's mind was on being home for Christmas before being sent to Vietnam.

By this time, we had received our orders, mine informed me that I was to report to Fort Lewis on 01\04\70 for transport to the replacement pool in Cam Ron Bay, South Vietnam. I had been in the army four months and one week. In that time my government figured I had gained enough knowledge and training to be sent to a war zone. I had a month of leave before I would go.

HOME FOR CHRISTMAS

I caught a bus from Fort Lewis down to Salem to see my parents and two younger brothers. After a couple of days with them I caught a ride to Santa Cruz to meet my girl and visit friends and relatives. I went by to see a friend, Randy, that I'd known since seventh grade. He was home for Christmas break from Arizona State University. When I arrived at his house, several others from our old group were there. The five of us sat around for a couple of hours while Randy's mom fed us lunch and made us feel welcome.

In the months since I had been away, we had all changed. The subject of the war came up, of course, and several of them suggested I go to Canada to avoid going. I could not do that. My dad and all my uncles had served in WWII. It took me off guard to know how many of my peers were not only against the war but also averse to stepping forward if being asked to serve.

For the rest of my leave I sought out more positive social situations. I spent as much time as I could with my girl. We traveled to Oregon with my sister and her husband in their Volkswagen bus to spend Christmas with Mom and Dad. While there, we enjoyed the warmth of family and friends. When we headed back south, it was with Mom and Dad's prayers that I would come home safe. Between my girlfriend and Mom and Dad I was reminded of my faith in God. Although I would constantly wander from the path, I had found a life sustaining faith. It would serve me well in the months to come and mature into a lifelong relationship with my Savior.

PART TWO

THE REPUBLIC OF SOUTH VIETNAM

We flew to Fort Richardson in Alaska then over the pole to Japan. It was a civilian airliner chartered by the Army, a no-frills flight packed with replacements. In Japan, we got off the plane just long enough for it to refuel and for us to be searched again for contraband and be given the chance to surrender anything not legal according to a long list posted on the wall.

There were no seating assignments. I found myself on the last leg of the flight setting next to a guy named Roy. He was headed back to Nam for a third tour. He was happy to learn that I was from California and knew what smoking pot was about. Roy said that if I stuck with him, I wouldn't be pulling any KP or filling any sand bags for our first few days in Nam.

Our flight landed at Cam Ron Bay and rolled up next to grey busses with wire mesh fastened over the windows. We had been briefed to offload as quickly as possible and to board the busses for transport to the replacement center at Cam Ron. The heat, the air, and the smell hit me like a hot wet blanket. We had all been issued new jungle fatigues before leaving the states. I was pouring sweat just from carrying my duffel bag from the jet to the bus. When our bus reached the replacement center, Ron and I stuck together. As soon as we were offloaded and a head count was taken, Ron and I slipped out of the crowd and into a crowd of guys headed home. We asked a couple of them (about our size), if they would switch their old jungle fatigues for our new ones. They were happy to make the trade and help out the New Meat. For the next three days we shuffled back and forth from mess hall to hanging out with the guys going home to a bunk at night. On our third day orders arrived for me. I was going up to Sally near Hue City to join the 101st.

The word was that they were seeing their share of fighting up there. I had been hoping for a nice quiet tour guarding a base somewhere on the back burner. At six the next morning a bunch of us boarded a C-130 to Danang and from there we caught a Chinook to Sally and checked into the 101st replacement pool. Our next four days would be P training or in-country training. I attended more advanced first aid classes and classes on mines and booby traps. We were shown how to use plastic explosive, C-4 along with TNT and DET cord. At night we had guard duty at one of the hundreds of bunkers that surrounded Camp Eagle. We learned to repel from a tower and from a helicopter. We attended lectures on various sexually transmitted diseases and were warned about guys who wound up dead from calling on the boom-boom girls. One of the lectures was about sappers, enemy soldiers trained to sneak in through the perimeter defenses at night and wreak havoc with our troops and blow up ammo caches. It was said that they could creep up on man and cut his throat without the guy next to him knowing it.

I was here, despite all my wishing and hoping and wanting something else. I was about to embark on an adventure not of my choosing. Like millions of guys before me back to Biblical times I was here on the threshold of war. I hoped, and I prayed that I could stand up to it. I'd had the best training in the world, (so I'd been told). I had the best equipment money could buy. I was here to face an enemy that had already been at war for years, an enemy that knew the terrain and had been living on it his whole life. I was trying to hold back my fear. My assignment showed up. I would be with Bravo Company 1st of the 502nd 101st Airborne Division.

A jeep gave me a ride over to my company area. I carried my duffel bag into the hooch that I was dropped in front of where I was met by the company clerk. He told me to drop the duffel bag, and he would lock it in a conex container. All I would need was the clothes on my back and my personal gear. The company clerk passed me off to the supply sergeant. The supply sergeant had a thousand-yard stare that you couldn't miss. He spoke slowly as he issued me my M-16 and had me repeat the serial number back to him. He then gave me a list of items and showed me to the next supply hooch. His voice was soft as he explained to me to pick from the magazines twenty-one of the best I could find, without dents. Load each one with 18 rather than the full twenty rounds, less likely to jam that way. He then left me there to fill out my list. The first thing I needed was a pack to carry it all in. There was a pile of them in the middle of the floor. As I sorted through them, I noticed that some of them had bullet holes and what could have been blood. I found one that was in relatively good condition and continued to load it with the rest of the items on the list. When I was just about finished, the supply sergeant stuck his head in the door and said, "There will be a deuce and half out front in five minutes." It would be my ride out to my company.

I climbed the tail gate of the deuce and half to find twelve guys already inside. The bottom and sides were covered with sand bags and they were packed in with about the same gear I had. I burrowed in to a place near the back, and we started off. After threading our way out of camp, we joined up with a convoy headed west. It was a warm, clear, late morning with just a little cloud cover. We wove through several villages and across a bridge where the view opened toward the mountains further to the west. I was thinking man, those are some steep, jungle covered mothers… and I hope I don't wind up there.

Our convoy came to a stop at Fire Support Base Birmingham. It sat on a hill overlooking the Song Tra Bong River. The base was home to about 400 troops. There were engineers, artillery and infantry. Their job was to try and stop the flow of NVA infiltration from over on the Lao border and from the A Shau Valley and to support operations in the surrounding area.

When I saw the size of the fire base and how well it was defended, I thought, yes, man, this don't look so bad. At that moment a lieutenant stepped up and said, "Get up there to that chopper pad. The next bird coming in will be yours." I humped the several hundred yards to the pad along with the other twelve guys. A Charlie model helicopter was just swinging around from the west and came in to a hover over the pad. The LT signaled for six of us to get on. I went in last and took a place next to the right door gunner. The pilot pulled in some torque, and we were air born. Concertina wire and the bunker line flowed under my feet as we picked up forward speed. We circled the base and gained altitude as the other birds joined in trail to our flight. The river passed under us, and the view of the jungle and the mountains in the distance were incredible. Bomb craters were everywhere, large ones with the jungle grown back around them, fresh new ones that looked like they were made yesterday in different sizes and ages. A testament written on the ground to the months and years that the war had taken place, I wondered if I could make it through my year.

Our bird was flying east and south toward some steep brush sided hills with old rice fields to the west and jungle to the south. We were on approach to Fire Support Base Arsenal, a slash of red brown dirt covering maybe two acres, surrounded by six rolls of wire and dotted with bunkers. Most of the sides looked so steep that if you dropped a brick it would roll to the bottom. The chopper pad was only big enough to land one bird at a time. We came hurling down in a cloud of dust as troops on the ground tried to keep their gear from blowing off the hill. The pilot balanced the load just touching the skids lightly as we un-assed the bird. We hunkered down as the rest of our flight repeated the process until troopers rushed to the last bird to pull off mail and resupply. As the last helicopter moved away the wind from the rotors died down, and my hearing started to return.

We walked back on to the chopper pad, and the 13 of us were lined up by size, tallest to smallest, like kids would do to choose players for sand lot baseball teams.

Lieutenant Whalen welcomed us to his platoon then turned us over to the three sergeants that were to become our squad leaders. They walked up and down in front of us, looking us over, asking us where we were from. Sergeant Gary told us that the thirteen of us were here to replace guys lost on the last several missions and that even with thirteen replacements our platoon would still be understrength. A platoon at full strength would have forty men. More replacements could possibly be expected at the next allocation in about two weeks.

I was the last guy at the short end of the line standing next to Arnulfo Flores. We were the last two to be picked by the squad leaders. We weren't really even picked. We were all that was left, and it was sergeant Gary's turn, so he got both of us. Before leading us away Sergeant Gary calls out to Sergeant Berry, "Hey, I'll trade you these two small guys for that big guy. I need someone to pack the machine gun." Sergeant Berry agreed and that is how I wound up being in his squad.

Sergeant Berry walked us over to our bunker to stow our gear and meet our other squad members. I was assigned to the first bunker to the right of the gate at the road that came up a finger ridge leading off to the northeast and back to Phu Bai. Jimmy Charles Mayberry, J.C., was from Louisiana. He carried the M-79 grenade launcher for the squad and had been in country for less than a month. Aaron Brass, called Bugs because of his thick glasses, was our M-60 machine gunner. He came into the squad at the same time as J.C. There were five of us newbies: Arnold Flores, Arnie from Austin, Texas, John Fouts from Tempe, Arizona, Kit Mellenger from Iowa, myself from California and

Beningo Santana, Benny, from Puerto Rico. Sergeant Berry brought us up to a complement of eight men. Over the course of the time I would spend with second squad, we would go to the field with as many as twelve and as few as four of us. We were to become veterans together, bonded together by the hardship of war in the jungle and by the boredom, terror, fear and humor of surviving in a tropical environment with a bunch of young Americans.

Sergeant Berry assigned me to be a rifleman, so the M16 was to remain my primary weapon for most of my time in country. I carried a basic load of 21 magazines, 378 rounds, and there would be several times when I would expend them all. A patrol was being put together of four men from first squad and four from second. We would proceed out of the gate and down the road checking it for mines, booby traps or signs of enemy activity for one thousand meters below the base. On the way back, we would be shown where an LP listening post would be set up for the night. The LP would serve as prior warning should the enemy approach the base at night. It didn't look like good duty to me.

We were inside the wire well before dark and were released back to our squads. Sergeant Berry reminded me about the land of steers and queers and made it clear that he liked to be constantly cracking crude jokes. Many of them directed at where one had called home before entering the big green. The artillery unit on the hill had a mess tent where we grunts were allowed to eat when we were on the hill. Four of us were sent to chow while the other four maintained security at our section of the bunker line. During chow, Sergeant Berry informed me that I would be the one from our squad to man the LP that night. I was to report to first squad after chow with my weapon and flak jacket to be briefed by Sergeant Gary and draw equipment.

I arrived at first squad and waited while the SSG was at the TOC (tactical operations center). I was introduced to Mike Corral, who was one of the replacements that came in with me that day. Two of the older guys there were Scotty Rocket and John Wayne. They were both on their third tours in Nam and had been to the Ashaw Valley, Nui Que and experienced numerous fire fights. They told Mike and me that we had been chosen because we were both from California. They warned us that the NVA would toy with us by yelling, "Fuck you!", before creeping in to slit our throats. Sergeant Gary arrived, issued us a PRC-25 radio and a case of hand grenades. We were given a call sign and told to break squelch every 15 minutes to indicate all clear. Our radio frequency would be monitored from the TOC at all times, but we were not to clog up the air calling in unless we spotted the enemy. Under no circumstances were we to use any light or to smoke while in the LP. We were given a password to use if we needed to get back through the gate in the dark. The gate was cracked open, so Mike and I could pass through the wire down the hill toward the LP.

The LP was a five-foot section of corrugated pipe buried in the ground with two layers of sand bags around the top and a grenade trap in the bottom. We passed it on our first try and had to double back to find it. We settled in and sent in our first SITREP (Situational Report) turning the volume down to cover the sound of the squelch when the hand set was pressed. While I stared into the darkness listening, Mike began to open up and prepare some grenades should we need them. This was done by grasping a string on the side of the cardboard tube that the grenades are packed in and pulling it separating the top, allowing the device to slide out of the canister. When the string is pulled, it makes a sound not unlike ripping paper. After hearing the sound six or seven times, things got quiet. We straightened the pins to get the devices ready to use, then sat back to stare into the night. A few stars broke through, lending poor illumination to the hillside below. Fog moved in and out making for no visibility most of the time. I had the handset to my ear and broke squelch at the required interval.

 A lot of whispered conversation crossed between Mike and I as the night wore on. I learned he grew up poor and rural, the son of a Mexican vaquero and an Irish mom. His last home was a ranch out of Hesperia, California, where his younger brothers and sister still helped the folks work with the owner's livestock. Extracting the information was tough and almost impossible to understand. Mike had all his teeth pulled in basic. The army had given him a new set of false teeth before sending him off to Nam, but the swelling of his gums hadn't gone down until he left the states, and now in order to talk he had to hold his upper in place which he did so with his tongue. As a result, all of his words came out with s's, so it made it even harder to understand him at a whisper. It sounded like his favorite phrase was, "The silly sucker said something, so I slapped him one." I got real good at understanding him, but it took a while.

Every few minutes one of the howitzers up on the hill above us would fire some rounds off into the night, providing support for some unit out in the bush. Several times mortar illumination lit up the hill behind us lending an eerie glow to the fog, kind of a pulsing as the flare swung back and forth beneath its parachute. Around midnight, things quieted down. Stillness crept over the hill, down the road and into the valley below us. We sat in LP our eyes straining at the fog and the darkness, our ears trying to capture any sound. Faa Que--- Faa Queee-, came a sound out of the darkness. Instantly, I was on high alert. My weapon was aimed downhill in the direction it seemed the sound was coming from. I could feel Mike tense up and hear his weapon click off safe. The sound came again Faa Que --- Faa Quee. I was reminded of what Scotty Rocket and John Wayne had said about the enemy calling out; "Fuck you," before sneaking in to slit our throats. I whispered to Mike, "What does that sound like to you?" He said, "Sounds shlike shom slil asminol." I whispered, "Sounds like some little animal. Yeah, me too." The sound came again and again from more than one direction and closer now. Mike whispered, "Ish shink I'llsh shrow a gershnade." At that I heard him pull the pin and stand up to throw the grenade down the hill. There was a comforting boom and flash and a sound like a steel spring being released. Then all was silent again for a few minutes. The sound came back again and was answered by a corresponding sound from another direction. This time I rose up and tossed my grenade into the darkness.

Our grenades had a 4 to 6 second delay from the time you released the spoon until the detonation. Throwing it down a steep hill it could easily roll past the intended target before going off. We began to hold the grenades for two seconds after popping the spoon and throwing the grenade. By doing this we could get the grenades to explode closer to us or get an air burst covering a larger kill zone.

We figured we'd been had by the old guys telling us that Charlie was out there yelling at us before sneaking in to cut our throats. Each time that noise came again out of the darkness we doubted the story. The instinct for self-preservation kept us from believing our own minds that said, "It is some small animal that makes that crazy sound." By morning we had thrown every grenade from the case we had started with. After dawn we took the empty grenade crate and our gear, radioed in that we were returning and presented ourselves at the gate. In the fog we were challenged for the password, and we were allowed back inside the wire. Sergeants Gary and Berry met us inside the bunker line and asked how it had gone. Mike held up the empty crate, and I said we threw every grenade. Gary and Berry had a good laugh. That was our first night, outside the wire and how we learned about the Fuck You Lizard. That's right a lizard.

There were a million chores to be done every day on a fire base. Each day the perimeter wire and defenses had to be inspected and repaired. Where wire had been cut by bullets or incoming rockets and mortars, we drove engineer stakes into the ground with sledge hammers and hung new wire or repaired what was there. We checked the placement and condition of claymore mines so that each man who pulled guard at night knew where they were and what areas of infiltration were covered. We made foo-gas in fifty-gallon drums then placed them at strategic places on the hill with a white phosphorus grenade and a claymore behind. We would load up the foo-gas further with waste shot bags (gun powder) from the artillery rounds. Below the base carved into the side of the hill was a garbage dump. Each day the trash was hauled there to be burned. A detail was assigned to do the burning and to guard the guys that were burning it. Supplies like cases of C-rations had to be guarded to make sure they were there when needed by the troops in the field. Feces burning detail was at the bottom of everyone's list, but we all had our turn at it. All this took place while helicopters brought in supplies blowing dust and anything that wasn't tied down around and down the sides of the hill. Helicopter resupply often required that a man disconnect the load while the chopper hovered a few feet above. This was always a dangerous job made more so by the static electricity that built up between the helicopter and the load. More than once I'd seen a trooper knocked on his ass by a static charge.

Water was lifted on to the hill in big rubber blivits. One load came in with two blivits that banged into each other in such a way that when they were released one of the blivits sprang loose and headed for the side of the hill. As it rolled, it began to bounce like a five-hundred-gallon water balloon. It cleared the landing pad; two guys in a fighting trench at bunker three went to ground when it passed over them. Nothing was going to stop it now. It ripped a ten-foot hole in the concertina wire and disappeared over the side of the hill. We saw it twice more as it reached the top of its upward bounce. Then it was gone, a testament to the American manufacturer who devised such a useful and utilitarian thing.

Patrols took place every day and most nights. We would travel light with just our weapons, water, claymores and a couple of cans of C-rations. Our patrols were made up with men from two squads, leaving behind half of each squad to rest up and man our positions on the bunker line. We would exit the wire with a patrol leader (usually a sergeant), a radio man, a machine gunner, assistant machine gunner, M-79 man and two to four rifle men who would walk point or rear security. The rifle men either carried extra machine gun ammo or claymore mines, besides their M-16 and basic load. We would check each other over to make sure gear was stored properly in order that we might move as quietly as possible.

My first couple of patrols seemed like just long boring yet terrifying walks, but I was learning how to move through the bush by day and by night. We sat in ambush a lot and learned to do it in the heat of the day with mosquitoes and spiders and ants crawling on us and at night when all the jungle sounds came to fill your ears with a thousand shrills and squeaks and chirps and those night stalker sounds. Something ominous would move through, and the whole jungle would go quiet.   I tried to hear above the rushing of my pulse pounding in my ears. It takes practice to really hear the jungle, to smell it, to taste it, to move in it like you own it. Those walks were the beginning of the infantrymen we were to become.

A few more replacements joined our platoon late in January. One was a guy named Ron who was transferred in from the 173rd. Ron was an E-4 with eight months in country when he joined our squad. We walked rear security together on a couple of patrols, and Ron began to take the time to school me on some of the finer points of staying alive. Ron wore his boots bloused to help keep the leeches out, so I did too. Ron kept his sleeves rolled down and buttoned to keep bugs out and to protect his arms from bugs or fire on a helicopter, so I did too. Ron wore a strap below each knee to keep his pant legs from filling with water when he forded streams and it kept less material exposed to snag on a bush, vine, or booby trap, so I did too.

After a couple of weeks of emulating Ron, our machine gunner, Bugs, started to call me Dapper Dan. Dapper Dan had been a river boat gambler during the 1800's and had a reputation for being a snappy dresser. When Sergeant Berry heard Bugs call me Dapper Dan, he said, "Don't you mean Diaper Dan?" The name stuck, no matter how much I didn't want it. I was Diaper Dan for the rest of my tour.

As a rule, we would rotate on to a fire base usually Arsenal or Birmingham for about one week out of four. This, however, was not a hard and fast rule. Sometimes we might come onto a fire base, get a hot meal and change of clothes, maybe a shower, and then go right back out to the bush.

PLATOON TO THE BUSH

We walked off Fire Base Arsenal as a platoon. My squad brought up the rear of the column with Ron and me walking rear security. We moved in a single file down the hill. This was our first time humping the boonies with full packs. Each of us carried twelve quarts of water to last us three days. With nine meals of C-rations and other gear no one had less than 80 pounds to carry. Some carried as much as 120 pounds. With the temperature hovering near a hundred degrees and humidity in the 90's, it was like walking in a sauna. At each break the medic would pass down the line trying to pass out salt pills. Who wants a nice fat salt pill with a drink of 100-degree water? We spaced out our interval to cross some open ground then closed it up when the brush got thick, and we started up hill. The hill was one of those where you think you are near the top at a place that flattens a little, but it doesn't. There is another steep spot then another. I was exhausted and when a five-minute break was called and when it was over, I couldn't get back on my feet. Ron stopped for a moment as he went by me. Remember we were rear security. He said, "Sometimes Charlie will follow the column to pick off a straggler or just to keep an eye on it." He then humped on out of sight up the hill. "God," I prayed, "please give me the strength to get up this hill." I hadn't caught up with the rest of the platoon when there was a big commotion coming from up the hill. I looked up from under my pack to see an unconscious trooper cartwheeling down the hill. I had to step aside to let him spin by or he would have taken me with him. His gear was strewn from the next level spot where he had almost made it to some thick brush about twenty meters below me where he and his ruck sack came to rest. I made it up to the level spot and shed my equipment before heading back down to help collect him and his kit. The medic was with him pouring salt water down his throat to bring him around. He was a big guy, and it took four of us to help him up to the level spot. The LT called for a break, so we put out security and broke for lunch.

Ron and me sat down on either side of the trail watching our six and pulled out some C's. The heat stroke dude was coming out of his funk, and we all had a little chuckle over it. Ron said, "Man, I thought for sure he was going to take you out like tenpins. You made a masterful stroke of getting out of the way." It wasn't funny, but what are you going to do? We humped hard and uphill for the rest of that day reaching the crown of the ridge at about 1800 hrs. The LT radioed back to break in place, so we set out security to the rear and flanks and enjoyed the view from the ridge.

Out in the bush we would, whenever possible, spend the night near or at the top of a hill. It was generally better defensively and if we needed artillery support, illumination, extraction or medivac there was a better chance of getting it. We would stop and find an NDP (Night Defensive Position) just before dark and eat some C's. A small patrol would go forward at this time and choose our real night defensive position. Just before dark, we would sneak into our night position, set out our claymores and go into our night routine. Most nights we would have three-man positions with one man awake on guard at a time. This way we broke the night into three, three-hour watches. The third watch would wake us up just before dawn, and we would move out and get away from our night position as soon as it was light enough to do so. We varied this somewhat to accommodate for night ambushes, weather, terrain and just because somebody got a hunch.

That next day we were moving by first light. The LT brought us to a halt at about 0800. We set up a perimeter defense and broke out C-rations. From here two squads would patrol out around the area in opposite directions looking for signs of enemy activity. The rest of the platoon waited here monitoring the radio as a ready reaction force to help should one of the squads come into contact with the enemy. Most of the time it was long hot humps through the brush or long hot days spent staring over the barrel of an M-16 at likely avenues of approach.

Sergeant Berry walked us out of the perimeter in the same direction we came in on that morning. Arne Flores was walking point, John was slack followed by Gordon, Bugs, JC, SSG Berry, me, then Ron. The slack man covered the point man's left and right as the point was focused on what was ahead. We moved slow and careful at a pace set by the point man. As we moved, we looked for sign trying to locate the enemy. We kept to the heavy brush below the brow of the hill, avoiding open areas or possible ambush spots. We stopped frequently to listen. We came across two old bunkers that were caved in and grown over. It was spooky, walking through Charlie's old back yard. As we moved, we would occasionally flush a bird or an animal that would go screeching or crashing away through the brush. You could hear all the safety's click off on our weapons as we froze in place or dropped to the ground. Arne found a trail that looked to be in use, so we called its location back to the LT. We were instructed to locate a good ambush site, set up and observe the trail until late afternoon. Sergeant Berry set us up with two claymores hidden and facing the trail. We spread out in a C shape behind the claymores so that our field of fire covered about twenty meters of trail. Sergeant Berry and JC were behind us to monitor the radio and guard our exit route, back the way we'd come in.

In the quiet the jungle sounds began to return, each of us sat in our own pool of sweat straining to decipher between the buzz of mosquitoes and natural noises and the sounds made by men moving up the trail. After several hours we could hear voices and the occasional clink of equipment percolating out of the brush from downhill. The pucker factor went way up as we glanced at each other and waited staring. Again, the sounds filtered towards us and again we gripped our weapons and waited to blow our ambush. We held our position until 1700 hrs. Ron and I were sent out to retrieve our claymores at the end of the trail nearest where the sounds had come from. As I disarmed the ambush, I had to fight back my fear. We had set there for three hours as tense as at any time in my life. I was so exhausted; I could barely lift my feet. It seemed like my nerves were going to jump out of my hands. We moved quietly to exit the area. Sergeant Berry called in a sit rep and let the platoon know we were headed back to their location. Arne took us back by a different route just in case we had been detected at some time during our patrol.

Back with the rest of the platoon we broke out the C's. The guys who smoked lit them up, and we were able to talk for the first time in eight hours. Bugs said that when we heard those noises in the ambush, he wanted to start hosing the whole hill down with his M-60. That got us all admitting that we were feeling some of the same urges and speculating on what we would have done if we had sprung our ambush. Sergeant Berry, back from reporting to the LT, just caught the end of the conversation. He said that we were all a bunch of momma's boy cherries and just lucky no NVA walked into our ambush. Ron said, "Berry is right, there could have been a whole company making those noises." We were just lucky, but it is good to be lucky.

The other patrol came back and reported that they had not seen anything but some old trails. They joined us to have chow before we would move out towards tonight's NDP site. We only moved a few hundred yards from where we ate chow to our NDP.

That was the night I learned the importance of burying your garbage deep. Some idiot had tossed a couple of C-ration cans into the brush between our claymores and us. Apparently, they had enough food left inside of the cans to attract varmints. I had last watch that night from two till six in the morning. As I sat there staring into the darkness, I wondered if there really was a company of NVA out there like Ron had suggested after the ambush. I began to hear a tinkling sound and a rustling in the dry leaves under the brush. The sound I estimated was only thirty feet or so in front of me. The night was pitch black with just a modicum of starlight filtering through if you looked straight up at the sky. My brain said, "It's only a small animal licking on a C-ration can." Then my other brain would say, "What if there is a sapper lying beyond the cans, using the noise to cover his movements? With each tinkle of the can, he creeps closer and closer." After hours of this, I wished the little varmint would either finish his meal or take the can with him. Our varmint ceased his torment just as the sun was beginning to rise. So, there was no chance of a positive identification. The coming year of jungle nights would give me plenty of opportunity to hone my skills of wildlife identification. At six we saddled up and moved out. During the process we quizzed one another about who threw out the C-ration cans. No conclusion was reached but Sergeant

Berry assailed us with a steady stream of epitaphs having to do with Worthless Cherry Boy Dipshits, bound to get him killed before his tour was over. Ron said the cans could have been there from someone else moving through ahead of us or they could have been NVA cans. He thought he could smell fish.

The platoon had been on the move from the time we left our NDP. The LT had found a landing zone where we could meet our resupply at 1400 Hrs. At 0800 we stopped for a break and broke into the last of our C's.

Each of us needed a gallon of water a day to stay hydrated. When there was natural water from rain or out of a stream or bomb crater, we would fill our canteens from that and put in purification tablets to make it potable. In this instance there was no water near our line of march, so it would come out on the resupply. This day we were drinking the last of the water we had packed off of FSB Arsenal. We sat around eating our C-ration breakfast and making coffee from little packets of instant poured into three-day old canteen water that came out of the river and was chlorinated at the fire base. The coffee and creamer powder that came with the C's couldn't cover the taste of the chlorine or the Halizone tablets used to make it potable. We adapted and overcame, First Strike Bravo. No Big Deal.

We humped the rest of the morning and secured the LZ by 1200 hrs. It was on a nice open hilltop where you could see all the way to the South China Sea to the East and over into Laos to the West. Our resupply bird arrived with perfect timing. Coming in to the green smoke, it touched down just long enough to toss out our resupply. The pilot pulled in pitch and went off to circle the area until he was called to return to pick up the empty water cans and mail bag. On the return trip anyone who was sick or had a bad tooth or needed to go to the rear for any legitimate reason, could get a ride in. We distributed the resupply and mail, filled our canteens and one-gallon water blivits, burned any waste and the C-ration boxes, loaded the water cans on the chopper when it came in and got out of there. We had just put on a big show out in the open, and we didn't want to be there if Charley was to show up in large numbers.

With fresh resupply we humped for two hours before taking a break. Our direction was bringing us to the West closer to Indian country. Our squad was in the back of the platoon. Ron and I were walking rear security. The point squad rotated each day and unless the going was so thick it had to be hacked through with machetes, the same point team would stay at it all day. Sometimes the point went forward fairly quickly. At other times they had to move very slowly due to terrain or feeling their way forward through triple canopy jungle or when we were in Charlie's backyard. When the line of advance stopped for any reason, every other man would assume a position to guard his side of the trail. The front machine gun would move forward to support the point team, and the rearmost machinegun would move back to support rear security. In this way we moved through the bush as quietly as possible like a caterpillar. We were moving down the ridge into much thicker jungle as night caught up with us. We formed up in a perimeter with the LT and his radio in the middle and the squads in three-man guard units facing out. Extra claymores and two more fighting positions were placed toward the trail we had made coming in. That night and the week following passed without any real excitement for our platoon. We were beginning to get to know one another and learning to operate in the bush as a squad and as part of the platoon. We became less prone to heat stroke. We became stronger and more adept at being in the Jungle.

On our eleventh day in the bush we were moving off the ridge system to go down into a steep canyon, cross a small river, and up the ridge on the other side. As we moved down towards the river, our squad was third squad back from the point. The LT and his RTO were between second squad and us in the line of march. Signs of enemy activity became more numerous as we got closer to the stream but mostly old stuff. We saw a fallen down hooch made from bamboo and cut trees that had weathered over. The LT and Platoon Sergeant decided that we would break at the river to refill our canteens and cool off. We were all at least eleven days from our last chance to get wet. When the river was reached, the first squad set up security on the near side. The second squad then passed through them crossed the stream and set up security on the far side. Our squad crossed the river, dumped our gear on the far bank and went to filling everyone's canteens and water blivits. When that chore was done, we got into the water to cool off.

I was lying on my back in the cool water, looking up at the clear blue sky through the trees, listening to the guys upstream from me talk in low voices. As I turned my gaze to look downstream, I saw the water exploding with little splashes that were walking their way toward me. I thought who is the idiot who is shooting into the water? In slow motion guys were getting up and running for their weapons. The security squad on the near bank opened up on the hill across from them. The little geysers of water stopped about three feet from me as I scrambled to my feet. I slipped on the muddy bank and fell just feet from my rucksack. Clawing at the grass and mud, I wrapped my hands around my M-16, and it was over. No more shots were fired from the hill. Two machine guns and an M79 and several hundred rounds of 5.56 had run off whoever the brave soul was that had fired upon us.

The platoon was formed up with LT and his RTO behind first squad. We started up the ridge toward where we had been shot at. Part way up the hill, we crossed a large trail about three feet wide that looked as though it had not seen use for some time. We followed the trail up the hill moving cautiously. On a shoulder several hundred meters farther on, the point team discovered two fresh hooches. There was an open spot in the jungle nearby that was probably used to launch rockets toward FSB Birmingham. From the open spot you could see the place in the river where we had been shot at. There was expended brass from an AK-47 or something that fired the same round in the clearing. We did a thorough search of the surrounding area for booby traps, equipment or Intel. The NVA had moved out. They left a clean camp all but for the brass from the shots they fired as they exited.

That was the first time I had rounds coming my way in Vietnam. Our antagonist was at about 400 yards, that's beyond the accurate range for most shooters with an AK, but still within killing distance if he had been lucky. Until this day, I can still picture myself in that water with the bullets stitching their way towards me. If his magazine had a few more rounds, the story might have been different.

Word came down to saddle up. We would continue up the ridge in the same line of march that we came down to the river in. It was slow uphill going through thick bush with a load of what we called "wait a minute vine." Wait a minute vine grows kind of like blackberry vine. Its tendrils are tough and fibrous and can be twenty feet long. It has thorns spaced along the vine every inch or so on two sides. The thorns hook back toward the base of the vine and are extremely sharp and hard. When one of these gets caught on your clothing or pack, forward motion stops. You must wait a minute, back up to take the pressure off the hooks and pull the vine off in the direction the hooks went in. Each member of the point team carried a machete so there were normally about three per squad. Often when someone would get caught by a vine a machete would come out in the hand of the guy behind, and he would separate his fellow trooper from the offending vine. When this would take place, it would make a peculiar sound. The hardness of the vine would often cause the machete to ring. With four squads and about twelve machetes we proceeded forward in a chorus of whispered, "Shit damn, zing! Mother, zing! Oh crap, zing! Son of a...zing!" Sometimes a trooper would become impatient and give a big jerk to free himself from a vine latched onto his rucksack causing the vine to whip around and find some exposed skin on his hands, arms or face. These could leave a series of holes or a nice long rip depending on how hard one pulled. The medic might see you at the next break, but mostly you just sucked it up and proceeded to march.

Huge spiders lived in the bush and spun their webs across any opening available. I remember stepping off the trail to relieve myself and walking into a huge web face first. This thing the size of my hand came, racing sideways from the web onto my face. I about broke my back throwing it into reverse and managed to back out of the web. The spider sat right there in the middle of his net as it sprung back and forth, wiggling his spikes at me. I found somewhere else to do my business.

We managed to move through the thicket of brush that held most of the wait a minute vine and continue up the ridge. The LT called for a stop when the point found a place to loiter and eat some C's. While we ate, the LT called in artillery on the site we had been fired on from. Sometimes, Charlie would come back to an area we had just left thinking it was safe. By registering the guns on that spot and calling in the location as a possible launch site, it could be fired on more readily in the event of a rocket attack from that vicinity.

Beningo Santana had a bayonet. At every break he was throwing it at something. It is amazing how comfortable we all became with him sticking it in the ground or in a tree near where we sat. He liked to sort of surprise you with it. He would give it a little flip, and it would be stuck in the ground between my feet or he could throw it with force past a couple of us lounging on our rucks and stick it in a tree. It seldom failed to stick. I asked Benny one time, "Why do you throw the bayonet so much?" Benny just said, "I am from Puerto Rico. I throw the knife!" Benny was a good dude. Always up for the mission. Never gave anybody shit. Tough as a jungle boot and always ready to laugh. He would mix instant coffee with cocoa powder to make coffee-coa the national drink of Puerto Rico. He would do any job or take any position in the squad, but he didn't like to talk on the flaking radio or be around flaking officers.

We moved from our loiter site into our NDP at dark and set up for the night. The following days went by a lot the same. Hot miserable humps through the bush or waiting in an ambush or patrolling by day and pulling guard or trying to see in the dark by night.

Most of our platoon had been in country for less than a month. Day by day we were being forged by the heat and the terrain to adapt to our new life. We learned a lot by watching the older guys. They stepped only where the other man stepped. In that footprint there was no booby trap. We learned from them the nuances of setting out claymores with a trip wire and a white phosphorus grenade in front to light up the kill zone. We would dig a small hole under the claymore and place a fragmentation grenade under it with the spoon being held down by the claymore. That way if the enemy was able to sneak past the trip wires to try and turn our mines around to fire towards us, they would be blown up for their efforts. When our point man would find an enemy booby-trap, he would lead us around it. Often, we would all get a look at it, so we came to know what to look for. Rear security would usually blow the trap in place using C-4 plastic explosive.

We encountered many booby-traps. Punji pits were probably the most common. As our tours wore on, we would discover many other more devious types that would contribute to thinning the herd. That may sound kind of callous, thinning the herd. Each time a man was wounded, or killed, or went to the rear for any reason, he might never come back. He got on the helicopter. (He Skied). A replacement would fill his spot from the replacement pool, and we would go on.

At first, I would ask about the guys that skied. "Are they ok? Will they be back out to the unit?" Most were ok, and some would come back. Others we would never see again, maybe because of their injuries, maybe because they signed up for another year with the army or made some deal to get out of the bush. They were gone, (Skied). The job on the ground was immediate. Grief or wondering about a friend took your mind off the task at hand. You load them on the dust off or the resupply bird, then immediately get your head back into staying alive. As the days went by, there came a winnowing effect.

Somewhere along towards the end of my first month with the platoon I became our squad RTO (radio telephone operator). I inherited the job from JC, I think, when he had to go to the rear to get a tooth pulled. I carried that radio for the next seven months. The dang thing weighed 23 pounds and had a four-pound battery. I always carried an extra battery. Being the RTO just was a fit for me. The RTO was always in on what was going on. Each radio was in communication with all the other radios in the company. (Five per platoon plus two for the flag about twenty-two in the company). We would have frequencies assigned for us to operate on. We could get on to the frequencies for artillery support or other forms of support as needed. Our call signs would change every week, to keep the enemy from figuring out who we were. Since our call sign designated not who we were as individuals but what unit or part of a unit we represented, most of the RTO's at the squad level had a nickname. By leaking out your nickname from time to time, other RTOs knew who you were by the sound of your voice. The nicknames were not universal nor were they officially sanctioned, but I operated that way and so did many RTO's at the squad level. My Radio name was Diaper Dan; the name Sergeant Berry branded me with. That is what most people called me and the only name most of the company knew me by. I became known also as Diaper or Dan. I answered to all of them. Most RTOs could go to sleep with the handset near his ear and awaken only when his call sign was used. He could do this even when his call sign changed each week. He could tell by the sound when a new radio entered his frequency. Every radio has a different sound, especially when it breaks squelch or is just tuned to a new freq. After living with that radio to my ear for a few weeks, I attained the skills.

I learned to call in artillery by plotting our location on the map and calling for strikes as the squad needed.

One time we were out in the thick triple canopy, just our squad. It had rained for a number of days, and every watch in the squad quit working. Sergeant Berry would ask me to call for a Tango Charlie, (time check), every few minutes. We had missed our extraction the last two days because of the weather. When it was clear over us, the birds were grounded. When the birds could get to us, we were socked in. We kept moving and hiding staying near enough to our LZ to get extracted should the birds become available. This was all causing us to use up a lot of radio time and a lot of Tango Charlie's. On one particular call the officer running the TOC asked, "What is the matter with you guys out there? You don't have a watch in the whole squad?" Sergeant Berry grabbed the handset from me and said, "Sir, we have been in the bush for eleven days straight during the monsoons. We haven't been resupplied for five days, and if the army wanted me to have a watch it would issue me one." We heard no more complaints, concerning our calling for Tango Charlie's.

THE REAR

The People in command thought it best to keep the line dogs out of the rear areas as much as possible. In the rear it seemed like every cook and clerk was wearing an army watch and had either a bayonet or a K-bar knife on his side. I guess that this was to stave off the enemy should they be attacked on the way to the PX (Post Exchange) or the EM (Enlisted Men's) club. We called anyone in the rear that hadn't spent their time in the field,

(REMF's). This stood for... rear echelon mother fuckers. In 1970 the racial tension in the rear area, at least in the 101st, was so thick you could cut it with a knife. There was a lot of black marketing, enough so that if you went into any town or village you saw the evidence of it. Goods that should be army issue were for sale on the street. Army chow was going in the back doors of restaurants in trade for cash or drugs or anything of value on the black market. Everything was available from hamburger to hand grenades. The attitude of those in the rear was different from those of us who went to the bush. REMF's could be consoled by antiwar sentiment. They could read about the protesters in the articles in print at the time and in the letters from home. There was a lethal cocktail of change taking place in the heartland. Antiwar sentiment, racial tension, women's liberation, sexual liberation and "Can we hold back communism?" All of these ideas were at a tipping point. The wives and girlfriends of twenty-year-old soldiers found it increasingly unpopular to be associated with a Vietnam vet. Of the thirteen of us that came into the platoon together, none of us came home before receiving a dear-john letter.

In order to keep my edge, I realized that I had to steer clear of thinking about or being exposed to all of the outside influences. When I went into the bush, my head had to be totally into the game. Charlie was out there waiting for us. He wasn't going home after a year. He wasn't going home until the war was over or he was dead. We were killing him at a rate of ten to one or better, yet he wasn't going away. He still waited for us outside of the wire.

About a month into my tour we came on to Fire Base Birmingham. We had been together long enough as a squad where we were starting to work together. Rather than walk off the fire base, we were being sent out by chopper. This was called a helicopter assault if we had artillery and or aerial rocket artillery and were firing our weapons as we came in. If we came in quiet, it was called an insertion. A flight of one or more birds would fly to an insertion point or LZ and drop us off as quietly as possible, often flying over more than one insertion point in hopes of confusing the enemy as to what LZ we got off at. We might go to the field as a company, as a platoon or as a single squad. Most often we would move to the edges of the LZ to secure it and check for enemy activity. When the area was secure, and all were landed safely we would move out on whatever mission was called for. These missions could be search and destroy, reconnaissance or a variety of other things.

The first mission that I remember being dropped in as a squad RTO was out of Birmingham as a platoon. Our flight took us west and a little north to drop us on a hill over by the border with Laos. Once we were on the ground, we moved out of the area to get some distance between us and our insertion point. We spent that first night in our NDP as a platoon. The next morning, we broke up into separate squads to patrol the ridge we were on, each squad searching an area for sign of enemy activity. Our main job on this mission was not to engage the enemy, but to find him and call in artillery, air support or a reaction force. We called it sneaking and peeking. It was the second day of the mission. We had been on the move since breaking with the platoon that morning. We came across sign of NVA several times, but it was old stuff nothing less than a couple of weeks old. We spent the hottest part of the day watching an old trail and enduring mosquitoes.

There is single, double and triple canopy jungle in this part of South Vietnam. The first canopy starts at the ground and grows

154

to about twenty feet. Where there is a double canopy, secondary trees top out at forty to sixty feet. The third canopy is as tall as two hundred feet towering over the under canopies below.

The ridge we were on was single canopy on the top then turned to double then triple canopy as it fell off into a narrow canyon. We broke for chow that evening after having the point team scout us out a place to NDP. We sat up for the night in three-man positions where we could monitor a nearby trail that ran below the brow of the ridge. It looked like it hadn't seen use for some time.

JUNGLE SOUNDS

My watch was from ten till two. I sat cross legged in front. Sergeant Berry sat behind my right side and JC behind my left. By reaching back to touch their feet, I could bring either of them awake immediately. To my front the hill began to fall away towards where our claymores and trip wires were set up, covering the trail below and protecting our sector of the perimeter. I sat there pulling my watch, straining to see into the various shades of pitch black. Sound sometimes carries a long way under the jungle, especially early in the morning. I could hear a few night sounds coming up from down below in the canyon. I heard a sound like an elephant. I whispered to myself, no, but then I heard it again, far off but distinct. I wiggled Sergeant Berry's foot. He was up sitting next to me in a second. "What is it?" I whispered, "I heard an elephant." He said, "What the ----, you heard a what?" I said. "I heard an elephant." Sergeant Berry sat up with me staring into the pitch black for maybe fifteen minutes before he laid back down whisper-mumbling something about stupid, cherry, messed up, misfit halfwits. No sooner than Sergeant Berry had begun to breathe regularly as he returned to sleep, I heard the elephant again. This time it sounded like more than one.

I waited straining my ears into the darkness trying to talk myself out of it. No, I heard it again I heard two elephants. I gave Sergeant Berry's foot a good shake. He popped up a little less quickly than the time before. He whispered to me, "What the ---- did you hear this time?" I whispered, "I heard two elephants Sergeant Berry, two this time." We sat there together listening as hard as we could to the pitch-black night. At last Sergeant Berry whispers, "When have you ever heard an elephant?" I said quietly, "At the Fleishhacker Zoo in San Francisco. My parents used to take us kids." "Oh," he whispered "The Fleishhacker, I might have known that a cherry ass nut job like you from California would have got a significant amount of his education at the Fly-shaker------- Zoo. You Idiot, if you wake me up again you better have an elephant by the balls." Sleep was mighty valuable out there in the jungle at night, and although I heard those elephants twice more before my watch was over, they sounded a long way off and going away.

The next morning JC said he didn't hear anything on the morning watch that sounded like an elephant. I was just getting ready to saddle up when our call sign came up on the radio. The word was that the NVA were using elephants to move rockets through the area. "Roger that," I said, "I heard them last night." Sergeant Berry ripped the hand set from me and said casually, "Roger, one of my people may have heard something, but we really weren't sure." They came back saying that they would get back to us; stand by. Sergeant Berry fixed his full attention on me. "Stand by, stand by, do you know what that means? You stupid flyshaker California puke. Stand By just means wait a minute, Sergeant. That's right, it means wait a minute while some officer REMF puke bastard decides if all ten of us, big strong

men, should go down in that canyon to look for your elephants."
Our call sign came back up the freak before Sergeant Berry
could finish admonishing me. Sure enough the orders came
straight from the TOC that we were to head down into the canyon
in an attempt to intersect the elephants trail then follow it. A
blocking force or gunships or both would come on line when the
terrain would allow it. We were to remain in contact with a sit rep
every fifteen minutes.

We saddled up and headed down into the canyon. John was
walking point when he came across the first trail. It was well
used and about twenty inches wide. We waited concealed,
listening for about five minutes before crossing to the other side
and heading down hill at an angle. Six hundred meters down the
bottom of the canyon flattened out. John hadn't gone twenty
meters before he came onto another trail. This one was four to
six feet wide with ten feet of clear overhead. There were elephant
tracks and elephant dung. There was a whole bunch of people
tracks, even a little set of wheel tracks. We stayed on our side of
the trail in the brush to keep any of our sign off of the trail. We
made our way along the foot of the canyon wall. Every few
hundred meters the point team would check our orientation to the

trail. We lost communication with the platoon and with the TOC. My radio just couldn't reach out of that canyon. In the afternoon the point team spotted a trail watcher, who may or may not have spotted them. We thought we heard the elephants several times from a long way off. Sergeant Berry whispered, "Let's get the ---- out of here." We needed to cross that upper trail at the top of the canyon before we could find a safe place to NDP, and we had to reestablish contact with the platoon and the TOC. We humped our asses off to get up out of the canyon. At the upper trail we stopped and listened for several minutes before crossing. The point team found a route back to the top of the ridge. It was getting dark. We found a place to NDP, set out our claymores and settled in to listen.

At our NDP site I put up the long john, (long antenna like a fishing pole) and was able to reestablish communications with the TOC. The company commander got on the hook with Sergeant Berry and wanted to know what had happened since this morning. Sergeant Berry informed the CO that we had lost the trail of the elephants late that afternoon and were out of communication, so we returned back up the ridge to find a safe NDP and get communications back with the rest of our platoon.

Just then LT Whalen our platoon leader broke in on the radio, so we now had full communication back. The whole story had to be repeated to them before they would get off the radio and let us eat some cold C's in the dark.

As we sat there in the dark, Sergeant Berry explained to me that there was more than likely a company or better in that canyon. We had come dangerously close to making contact with them. Shortly after the point team saw the trail watcher, we heard whistles. That would have been the NVA signaling to their people, probably letting them know we were in their AO. There is no way in hell that we were going to take on an NVA company or even hold them off until help could arrive in that canyon at night. "Those who fight and run away, live to fight another day." Sergeant Berry had been in country for ten months. He ought to know.

We remained on full alert all of that night. We kept hearing noises coming up out of that canyon. The next morning, we joined up with the rest of the platoon and made for an LZ to get resupplied. After we had secured the LZ, we were able to kick back and relax just a little. It was the first time in three days that we could talk in a normal voice without whispering. I went over to where Mike was set up and shot the shit with him for a while. His squad had been further down the ridge from us on a peep and sneak. By the sound of things our squad had most of the excitement. Resupply came in. We packed up and left the LZ. The platoon would NDP together that night. Word came down that we would be patrolling into the canyon the next day. At first light two squads were sent out in opposite directions to patrol up and down the ridge. Our squad was sent up the ridge. We had gone maybe five hundred meters when Arny spotted a booby trap. There was a small limb sticking into the trail. Had Arny brushed it aside, it would have released a four-inch mortar hung in a tree. The squad backed away from the site while the trap was disarmed by setting it off. We reported in to the LT, and he recalled us to his location. When the other squad came in, they reported that the ridge below us had been booby trapped, also. They had disarmed a grenade with a trip wire. These guys had come onto the ridge our platoon had been all over the day before. They had bobby trapped in front of and behind us, and we had never seen them. I'm thinking, who are these guys and what are my chances of surviving a year of this?

At this time the enemy still had no face for me. He was a ghost that moved around by night setting traps for us to spring by day. I was scared, sometimes even terrified. Would I be able to do my job when called upon? Would I curl up in a ball and cry while frozen in place by fear? We had a couple of close calls. I had yet to see the real horror of war. For the next several days Sergeant Berry kept referring to me as Fleishhacker and coming up with elaborate stories, starting with, "If you ever need to know anything about elephants?"

All of the rest of Bravo Company came out and joined us on the ridge. Platoon size patrols were run down into the canyon and around the area over the next few days. As I recall, there was a booby trap casualty in one of the other platoons. The guy skied with a million-dollar wound. That is what we called a wound that got you out of the bush but wasn't fatal or crippling. The NVA had moved out of the area leaving behind some booby traps to be sure we knew they had been there.

We continued to operate as a company over the next several weeks. When you are humping the brush in a company you are one guy in a line of over a hundred. Unless your squad is on point you are packing your load looking at the ruck sack of the guy in front of you and hoping for some kind of relief from the mind numbing, back breaking labor of keeping the pace. With a whole company of grunts, you are bound to find some comic relief.

THE SLOTH

One of the grunts in another platoon had a sloth that he had bought from a kid in a village. The sloth traveled everywhere with him for several months. The sloth would ride on top of his ruck sack with his front end draped over his helmet and his long toe-claws hooked on the rim. As they moved, they created syncopation, so that it looked as though the sloth was humping the guy's head. Sloths have those big dreamy eyes that kind of stare off into nothing, lending to the post orgasmic image. The pair displayed at all times. You just had to smile when you saw them. There were four lieutenants and a captain that knew about them. They brought so much pleasure to anyone that humped the boonies with them. No one wanted to bring it to an end. I'm guessing the sloth was pretty young when first bought, but at some point, it returned to the wild. For the rest of my time in Nam, I would hear the phrase, "Horney as a three-toed sloth,"

163

and chuckle at images it conjured up and revel in the rebellious nature in all of us that had the opportunity to enjoy them.

Bravo Company was air lifted on to Birmingham after three weeks in the bush. Our platoon held down six bunkers looking downhill through the wire above the Song Tra River and a dirt road that followed it west toward the border with Laos. My squad was in bunker twelve. We arrived on the hill in the late morning and got settled into our positions before noon chow. We had been eating C-rations exclusively while in the field and looked forward to a real cooked meal. Half of us at a time were able to leave our positions and go to chow. That put about sixty filthy grunts in the mess tent at a time. As we moved through the mess line with our trays, the mess cooks stepped back trying to get a breath of air. None of us had bathed in three weeks. Nobody but a grunt could stand to be in there with us.

A company of engineers on the hill had built showers fed by a water wagon that had to be filled by hauling it down to the river and pumping it full, then hauling it back up. That afternoon we all got showers and a fresh set of jungle fatigues between trips to the river pulling security for the water wagon.

Washing the stink off after three weeks was like a rebirth. I was dripping dry when I picked up my soiled jungle fatigues to get the stuff out of my pockets. When I got them in my hands I just about puked from the smell. By this time, I had quit wearing socks and underwear. They just held moisture next to my skin, and I found I did better without them. Most of us carried a sweat rag, (a small OD towel or soft cotton T shirt material). I would rinse it clean at any stream crossing, bomb crater or puddle. They were hard to come by, coveted by grunts.

Duty on Birmingham was what we considered "getting over" compared to being in the bush. We pulled guard duty from the fighting positions near the bunkers at night. Next to our bunker sat a duster (a tank with a twin forty-millimeter cannon mounted on a turret). A little section of the bunker on that side had an enclosed fighting position with a single shot bolt action rifle mounted on a monopod. A starlight scope was mounted on the rifle to watch over the river at night. There was a hand set in the position connected with the duster next door. If the guard saw a sampan coming up or down the river, he would load a tracer round into the rifle and get the duster on the horn. The guys in the duster would direct their rounds to follow the tracer to the target, and the river traffic would disintegrate under a hail of forty-millimeter-high explosive.

Guarding the dump was one of the jobs grunts did. Two men would be detailed to keep an eye on the villagers that came there each day to scrounge through what the army didn't want. We would inspect whatever goods the locals were hauling out to make sure nothing was leaving that could be used against us. The dump was fenced in. We would station ourselves at the gate where everyone had to walk past us to get out. I only remember women of all ages doing this work, from little girls to old mama sans. We would rig up a sun shade, tied to the fence next to the gate. The mama sans that had babies would make a sun shade near us and leave their babes there with us while they went off to scrounge. We were never asked to watch them. They were just placed within a few yards of us on a mat they could crawl around or sleep on. There were rats in the dump that supported a population of snakes, some poisonous. I guess they figured that since we were sitting there all day anyway, we might as well keep an eye on the kids.

When a truck would arrive from the fire base, the mama sans would gather round all excited to see what was going to be dumped off next and to get first pick at any valuable assets. Several times a day, a fight would break out between the women over who got to the good stuff first. There were times we had to intervene to restore order. No matter who we sided with, the rest of the mama sans would get mad saying, "You numba fucken ten thou GI!" They would cuss us out and laugh. Their betel nut-stained teeth showing through their smiles. If one of the babies started to cry, its mother would come and care for it taking it to her breast without hesitation. She would chat with us in broken English as a thousand flies crawled and buzzed everywhere on her and her baby. In the afternoon the dump would shut down for the day. The ladies would all grumble at us as they headed out the gate. They had several miles to walk back to their village, carrying their goods on their heads or in woven basket packs that seemed much too big for them. They went on their way laughing and talking like they were returning from a day of shopping.

Mike and I were assigned to man the OP (observation post) that looked north, east and south from Birmingham. It sat on a finger that ran from the northeast about one third of the way up the hill. It was about ten by ten with sand bag walls up about four feet. Four posts supported a beam and runway mat roof with several layers of sandbags over that. The roof overhung the OP by about three feet all the way round, so it was always shaded. Being placed where it was, it caught a little breeze off the river. With a good set of binoculars, you could see for miles. We had a radio at the OP to call the TOC should we see anything of interest. One of us would scan the area while the other rested. Guys from the platoon would stop by sometimes just to shoot the shit and enjoy the most pleasant place on Birmingham. Officers were almost never seen there. An hour or so into our watch Scotty and John showed up. We called them "Scotty Rocket" and "John Wayne." Later on, I found out, they served at Hamburger Hill on their third tours. They were both great soldiers and yet always found a way to get in trouble. The talk wound around to girls at home, and Scotty got to telling us about his last trip to the states. He flew into San Francisco. There were antiwar protesters waiting for returning GI's at the airport. A couple of guys got spit on and a fight broke out with the antiwar crowd. When he went to see his bride-to-be, she was in bed with the guy she bought her drugs from. Scotty canceled the allotment to his girlfriend, re-upped for Vietnam, and took a month leave in Thailand. That was almost two years before. Since then he'd been on leave four times, but never gone home. John's story was a lot the same. He was airborne, stationed in Germany and volunteered for Vietnam nearly three years ago. On their second tours, Scotty and John wound up in the same squad with the first of the 0 duce. They spent their R&Rs together drinking and partying in Thailand or Australia. Both had been busted from sergeant several times and refused to be squad leaders after that. Both of them had been decorated numerous times and were highly respected for their skills in the field. John and Scotty were incorrigible as far as military record is concerned, but they were the kind of guys you wanted in your squad if the shit hit the fan.

I had a picture of my girlfriend and pulled it out for John and Scotty to see. Scotty commented that she was a nice-looking girl, and he would be glad to go by and visit her for me being as he would be going back to the world in just thirty-eight more days. He was a two-digit midget, less than ninety-nine days left in country. The old timers were always giving the fresh meat a bad time about their girlfriends. I guess it kind of softened the blow from the inevitable breakup that was bound to come. Scotty and John planned to end their tours and meet up in Thailand. They had been buying gems there and mailing them back to the states and planned to finance their return home in style. All they had to do was to live through the next thirty-eight days.

After spending all afternoon in the OP, Mike and I had the night off to sleep. There was going to be a movie at the mess tent, so we decided to take it in. The movie was Mash, which we had heard was banned because of antiwar sentiment. Somehow a copy of it was at the mess tent. So, why not? Mike and I found a seat on a table near the back looking over the heads of the guys in front. Each reel of film had to be rewound before the next one was played, so a guy held a flashlight for the projectionist as he changed reels or worked on the machine when it would jam up. When this would happen, we would yell and scream and give the guys as much shit as possible until the film was running again. In the movie there were several instances of incoming mortar and artillery rounds. The projectionist had just finished another round of working on the projector and was enduring more of our banter. The cover on the projector slapped closed. The flashlight went off, and the film came back on just as the first mortars hit. Over the sound of the movie came the crump of mortars. I hit the floor and began crawling for the exit. As I cleared the tent, I could see flashes where mortars and rockets were landing inside the perimeter. I knew my place was in the fighting position to the left of bunker twelve. I had left my weapon with my gear at the bunker. That was the first and only time I'd be caught without my M-16. It was about two hundred yards to my fighting position. I ran and crawled taking to cover as the barrage rained down. I prayed the whole time. "Please God, let me get back to my weapon." I made it back to the bunker, retrieved my M-16, three bandoleers of ammo and made my way to the fighting position. Arney Flores was already there firing his weapon down the hill. I popped up next to Arney and fired a full clip down the hill then reloaded and did it again. Loading the third magazine I got myself under control. Peeking my head up over the sand bags I waited for a target of opportunity. There were still mortars coming in, but they had shifted their fire towards the other side of the hill. Our mortars started to fire illumination giving us a look at what was out in front of us through the wire. We could see movement out past the range of our claymores at the edge of the mortar illumination. All the fighting positions in our sector were firing down the hill. Only a few rounds came back in our direction. The mortar illumination shifted to the other side of the hill where the in-coming was now concentrated. Our side of the hill got dark and quiet. We had a few pop flares that we could fire off if we needed immediate illumination, but they don't last as long or light up as big an area as mortars do. Every few minutes, illumination would be fired on our side of the hill allowing us to get a look out in front of our positions. The noise coming from the other side of the hill let us know that the main attack must be concentrated on that side.

Jimmy Charles yelled from the other fighting position, so I moved over to help him moving back along the trench through the bunker and out the other trench to his fighting position. When I got to him, he asked if I could hear anything. He thought that he could hear movement coming from a little gully that ran up the hill to the right of his position. I yelled back over to Paul who was at the other fighting position to get ready to fire up a pop flare. Pop flares are about fourteen inches long and an inch and one half in diameter. They have a cap on the end that when removed and placed over the opposite end arms the flair. By aiming the flair up and slapping the bottom, it fires a small rocket with folding metal fins to an altitude of several hundred feet. When it reaches the top of its flight white phosphorus pellets begin to burn providing a few seconds of illumination. I crouched in the trench halfway back toward the bunker. When Paul fired the flare, JC and I would take the gully under direct fire from two directions. As the flare went up, JC and I rose and fired our M-16s towards the gully. We couldn't see any enemy movement. Just as the flare was burning out, another flare went skyward at an odd angle and Paul began yelling, "I'm hit! I'm hit!" Leaving JC there to cover his position, I made my way back to Paul. In the dark I could feel blood from his helmet down to his chest. I started dragging him back to the bunker and yelling for the medic. I helped Paul onto a bunk in the bunker just as the medic pulled the poncho aside that covered the entrance. Boots, the platoon medic, put a light on Paul's face revealing blood, powder burns and gashes that ran from his lower lip to halfway up his nose. I exited back to the fighting position we had just vacated to maintain security on our section of the hill. Gun ships were circling the hill by now, discouraging Charlie from any further attempts to penetrate our perimeter. We remained on 100% alert for the rest of the night. There was sporadic firing from positions farther around the hill, but no more movement that we detected near us that night.

The next morning on the way to chow I went by the medical tent to check on Paul. He was up moving around with his nose bandaged the size of a medium zucchini. As it turned out, what he was hit by was his own pop flare. He had prepared an extra one to fire and laid it on the sand bags that ringed the fighting position. Somehow or another, he had knocked the second one off the sand bag. It fell to the bottom of the hole and discharged. Upon leaving the tube, the small rocket deployed its steel fins just as it met up with Paul's nose. The medics had cleaned off the powder burns from the propellant and stitched his nose up. He wound up walking to the mess tent with me. He got a lot of strange looks and everyone wanted to know what happened. How much explaining do you want to do about a self-inflicted pop flair wound? The medic told Sergeant Berry to give Paul light duty for a couple of days.

As I recall, there were no KIA's that night. Several medical evacuation helicopters came in at first light and hauled some guys to the hospital in the rear. The artillery unit lost a couple of guys to mortars and the infantry to mortars and small arms fire. Three NVA dead were pulled from the wire on the other side of the base. Numerous blood trails and drag marks testified to enemy casualties. Patrols were sent out to check the perimeter. Those of us who weren't patrolling began repairs to our perimeter defenses. The ordinance we had expended the night before had denigrated the wire and tangle foot in front of our positions. All around the perimeter there were guys stripped to the waist swinging sledge hammers, driving engineer stakes in the hundred-degree heat. Mules (small four-wheel drive carts) brought out rolls of concertina wire and stakes. We packed claymores, pop flares, grenades and machine gun ammunition up the hill from the ammo dump to refortify the hill and restock fighting positions and bunkers. We reloaded all of our magazines for our personal weapons, and we sharpened the blades of our knives.

Sergeant Gary had taken a patrol out in front of our sector of the hill. He came back to say they had found blood trails leading away towards the brush along the river. We checked the bunker and fighting positions again making sure we would be ready if they came again that night. By this time, everyone had been awake for more than a day. All of this had taken place while helicopters were coming and going blowing dust and debris around the hill. Hundreds of artillery rounds were fired from within our perimeter in support of units in the field as well as to break up troop movements around the base. Add to all that the smell of gun powder, blood, sweat and burning fecal matter. Oh! And don't forget the sound track of, Led Zeppelin – "Whole Lotta Love (Babe I'm Not Foolin')"- screeching out of a portable tape player or the squawk of the PRC-25 tuned to the company net.

The Artillery men worked their asses off. Helicopters would bring in sling loads of artillery rounds. They were packed in cases that had to be broken down, and the rounds stored near the guns. The powder load of the rounds was adjusted for the weight of the round and the distance it would have to travel to its target. The fuses for each round had to be set according to the type of round and what it was supposed to do when it reached its target. Did the troops on the ground need an air burst to kill the enemy above ground? Did they want the round to explode on contact or should the round penetrate before going off? There were different kinds of rounds, HE (high explosive), probably the most common, then WP (white phosphorous) to burn things up or mark a target, illumination rounds, then there were flechette, thousands of tiny little darts. Unit after unit would call for their support, and those guys would stick by their guns. Sometimes they would keep it up for so long that they would almost disappear behind their piles of spent casings and ammo crates.

Often all day and all night they would be called upon to support missions in the field.

NVA units would probe our perimeter at night to find a soft spot or just to keep us up all night to wear us down. After three or four days of 100% alert at night and repairing defenses all day everyone's nerves were on edge. You got to where you wanted them to show up because you wanted to kill them.

A few South Vietnamese civilians were permitted on the base, one was a barber named Bien. Several days a week he could be found up by the TOC plying his trade. A line of guys would be setting on a sand bag wall shooting the shit while Bien cut hair with scissors and a pair of those old clippers where you squeeze the handles. Bien also used a straight razor. He would bring up a big tea kettle from the mess hall, put a hot towel on your face and with a little soap give the closest shave most of us ever had. All the while he'd be jabbering away in Vietnamese like we understood every word he said. On the one hand, it felt so wonderful to be pampered and catch a little of that old-time barber shop feel, while on the other, here was this gook scraping at your neck with a straight razor. When you stood up from that folding chair, the breeze on your face and neck made you feel like a new man. As I made my way back down to bunker twelve, the sweat ran onto my freshly shaved neck as a helicopter blew another cloud of dust over me. I began to wonder if the barber might show up at somebody's fighting position tonight with his straight razor.

When we occupied bunker twelve upon coming onto the hill this time, there was a sign over the entry way, it read, "Don't Kill the Snake." A large black snake about six feet long occupied the bunker with us. This was a great blessing because most of the bunkers had rats. When sleeping in the bunker, it was not unusual for a rat to climb over you while going about his nightly business. With the snake there, the rats found another place to live. However, it could be every bit as disconcerting to come awake in the pitch black to have a six-foot snake crawling over you. The snake seemed to know that we were bound by a common enemy not to hurt him. On cold nights when the fog from the river would cool the air, he would curl up near enough to steal some body heat from a sleeping GI.

One morning, John Fouts, woke up next to the snake, and a new joke was born. John is the horniest GI on Birmingham; he slept with a snake last night! There was no end to the lengths we would go to bring some humor into our daily existence. One hot afternoon on Birmingham, we were sitting around killing time waiting for enough helicopters to become available to fly us back out to the field. We would often eat our C-rations after heating them over a burning piece of C-4 plastic explosive. It was an ideal heat source. It burned extremely hot and without smoke. It was always available. Most of us carried two one-pound blocks of it. Bug's was experimenting with some of the stuff a few yards from us while we ate. He took a piece about the size of a dime, lit it on fire, then threw an empty mortar box on top of it to make it explode. Bugs, was about six feet tall with thick glasses. He was skinny but well-muscled with a thick neck from carrying the machine gun and a hundred rounds of ammo hanging off him. He was seldom a joker, but I guess this was his day. He was having a hard time getting the ammo box to hit squarely on the C-4 to make it explode. He was on his fourth or fifth attempt when he decided to up the ante. Returning to the block of C-4 he tore off a chunk about the size of a golf ball. This stuff has seven times the explosive power of dynamite. He placed the small globe on the ground near a sand bag wall that was the side of a bunker and set fire to it with his Zippo. Bugs then proceeded to climb onto the bunker with the mortar crate in hand. Standing with his boots six feet above the ground, he brought the crate down from an overhead position, directing its mass perfectly centered towards the flaming ball. This time his efforts met with success. The small explosion completely disintegrated the crate. Sending shards of wood and pieces of metal hardware skyward all-around Bugs. The look of surprise on his face as he peered at us through his smoke-rimmed glasses would never leave us. Except for his pride, he was unhurt. We laughed so hard our sides were splitting. From that day forward if you wanted to get a fire going under Bugs you only needed to refer to him as our "explosive's expert".

Our flight assembled and ferried the entire company to the field. We were inserted on a hill east of Birmingham and set up a hasty perimeter before moving out up the ridge line. After humping several thousand meters we set up at the top of the ridge for the night. Through the trees that ringed that ridge we watched tracers pour on and off of a fire base several miles away. We sat there in our positions listening to the sounds of battle far off hoping that the enemy would be too busy to bother with us tonight. The next morning found us moving east down the ridge. We entered triple canopy jungle several hundred meters before reaching a stream at the bottom of the hill. Our platoon was near the center of the column as it inched its way down into the steep valley and up the other side. As my squad moved across the stream, I noticed places along it that looked as though someone had sat or kneeled to wash or collect water. We moved now up hill on a well-worn path. Just as I thought I would pass out from exertion, a break was called for. I positioned myself to cover our right flank and pulled out a canteen while listening to the hand set on my PRC-25. As I caught my breath, I was scanning the brush in front of me. That's when I realized we were on a stone stairway. Away from the center of the stair the steps were more angular; down the middle they were so worn away as to be barely recognizable. In places there was no sign of them so completely had the jungle swallowed them up. As we continued up the incline, we saw more signs of the ancient civilization that had occupied this ground. At a bench farther up there was a courtyard of stones with walls of matching cut stones on two sides. At one end was a huge stone head maybe twelve feet high. It looked across the courtyard at the remains of a structure, possibly a temple. Many of the stones were carved with reliefs of symbols unrecognizable to me. All of this existed under two-hundred-foot-tall teak wood trees that wound their roots around. Vine bamboo hung in the shorter trees and lower branches closing out the sun, creating a spooky, silent reverence as we passed.

We were moving very slowly and cautiously, every man as quiet as he knew how to be. We could hear a sound like someone chopping down a tree. We would hear ten or fifteen rhythmic chops then a pause as if to rest then another round of chopping, then another rest. The company came to a halt while a patrol was sent forward to check things out. In the meanwhile, the chopping noise continued though the rest periods seemed to become longer and more frequent. Regular jungle noise seemed undeterred by the chopping sound. The patrol that went forward was late getting back. They had not found the source of the noise, nor had they found any sign of recent enemy activity. Dark was upon us, so our orders were to NDP in place. A guard post was set up at the two ends of the company facing up and down the trail. Each position had an M-60 machine gun behind an array of four claymores with trip flares in front of that. There were nearly a hundred of us strung out between those two positions. I was to pull the watch from midnight to three with Pop Flare Paul.

We arrived at the guard position together at 1200 hrs. The guys coming off watch reported no activity but animal noises. Paul and I sat within arm's reach of each other. Every couple of minutes he would whisper to me in his Boston accent, "You hear that?" I was straining my ears up the trail and into the jungle trying to make sense of the sounds. We kept hearing what kind of sounded like footsteps mixed with a low talking mumble and a faint chirping noise. "You hear that?" Paul would whisper. I'm reasoning that this is some kind of animals, but they are closer than our claymores, so how did they get past our trip flares? Can these animals be that smart or is this the enemy probing our defenses? How can they be this close to us? Its pitch-black night, so even if you look straight up, no light penetrates the jungle. "Can you smell that?" Paul whispers. I could smell something like sweat and fecal matter very faintly. Whatever was in front of us, there was more than one. The sounds of leaves moving, and soft foot falls grew closer. There came a point where I could hear breathing that wasn't coming from me or Paul. I tried to control my breathing and heart rate to allow me to hear. Whatever it was, it was directly in front of me now, and it was breathing in sync with me. When I would take a breath, it would take a breath, and when I would exhale, it would exhale. This went on for what seemed like an eternity. My mind went to the guys sleeping behind me and my duty to guard against the enemy then swam back to my reasoning that these were some jungle animals making their way through a platoon of grunts in the dark. "You hear that?" Paul whispered again. My heart was pounding as I held my breath straining to make sense out of what was right in front of me. Finally, I let out a huge breath along with a low growl. The animal in front of us let out a similar breath followed by its growl and retreated back into the night. Paul and I whispered back and forth congratulating one another on our restraint while the adrenalin drained off. The remainder of our watch was uneventful. We were relieved at 03:00 and got some sleep until wake up.

The platoon was moving at first light. Again, we were moving up the hill we had started up the day before. We had only moved a few hundred yards when the point man fired a three-round burst. The platoon went to ground with my squad back at rear security. It came over the radio that the point had been surprised by a family of Rock Apes that crossed the trail. There was no blood to be found, so it appeared the apes got away safely. This was one of many encounters with the animals that populated South Vietnam. Each day and night my senses became more acute as I came to be accustomed to the sights, sounds and smells of the jungle. It has always been a curiosity to me how there were so many animals that moved around at night, yet so few of them tripped our trip wires. Pigs were the exception. We had several occasions where they blundered into our ambush sites at night.

THE BUG OUT

We had just been resupplied by helicopter. Mail came out as well as fresh jungle fatigues and sundry packs. After humping all morning to reach and secure the LZ, the platoon was basking in a break while we waited for the birds to return to pick up anything headed to the rear. One of the squads at the downhill side of the LZ spotted a trail watcher. As soon as we could, we packed up and got out of the area, putting as much distance as possible between us and the LZ. Before moving into our NDP site, the last squad in the line of march dropped off four men to watch the trail behind us. When later they caught up with us, they reported that they could hear movement behind us but that no NVA were seen. There were strange sounds in the bush that night, and several of the guard positions reported hearing what sounded like equipment bumping as the enemy moved around outside our perimeter. By 04:00 the LT was convinced that a sizeable force of NVA had moved in around us. Every man was awakened, and we got ready to bug out. Just before sunrise, we would have a mad minute where all our claymores would be blown, and every position would fire two magazines to their front. At this point the squad at the uphill side of the perimeter would move out uphill straddling the ridgeline. The other squads would follow them out with the last squad pulling rear guard. Our squad was last out. Some screams could be heard when we blew our claymores. There was very little return fire. We exited the NDP site as fast as we could and humped all morning. We kept calling in artillery strikes behind us to keep the enemy from closing in on the rear of the column. Along with the impacting artillery, we were in the midst of a lightning storm. The lightning was hitting so close you could hear the steam coming off the trees and the ground when it struck. The point man hit a trip wire connected to an explosive device that got him and the man behind him. We needed to move to an LZ to get them on to an evacuation helicopter. There happened to be a useable LZ farther up the ridge we were on, so we started in that direction. All the while, we are calling in artillery behind us to slow the progress of whoever is behind us. The front of the platoon got onto the LZ and secured it while the rest of us were still strung out down the trail. A break was called for. We had been on the move since 05:30 going uphill as fast as we could go while under sporadic fire in a lightning storm. It was now 14:00, and none of us had eaten in that time. The medical evacuation had to be called off while yet another lightning storm struck our hill. This time it struck one of our platoon mates in another squad. I picked up word of it over the radio. As the storm moved away, the sky cleared, and our medivac got in. I came walking onto the LZ just in time to see it heading east towards the South China Sea. Setting on the ground at the edge of the LZ next to where I walked was a boot still smoking. It had been blown off the guy struck by the lightning. It was a weird image, that smoking boot. It kind of symbolized the way we all felt. Chased around by an invisible enemy who had been inflicting casualties on us, we were exhausted and mad as hell. Then things got better. Someone in the rear heard about our situation and sent us out a hot meal - pork chops with mashed potatoes and gravy and corn along with two beers per man. I sat there against my ruck-sack chewing on a pork chop and drinking a Schlitz. I could see all the way to the South China Sea. I was alive and unwounded, and I had a feeling the Lord might preserve me through this experience. As I looked around, I saw that most of the guys were still mad. Mad at the enemy. Mad at the army. Mad at the politicians. Mad about racial strife. Mad about the heat and cold and rain and mud and mosquitoes and jungle rot and the guy dating their girlfriend and mad. Just plain mad. Mad enough to kill.

I smelled them pork chops, and I had another sip of that Schlitz and somehow right there I could see above it. I had decided that if I was the best I could be, I might see the end of a year here and if not, I've seen the South China Sea from the top of this mountain. We could choose to be miserable or we could choose to be happy.

With our wounded inbound and our bellies full, word came down to saddle up and move off the LZ. The platoon moved farther up the ridge line in search of the enemy. At sunset we moved into an NDP site and prepared to spend another night in the jungle. When conditions permitted, we would set up hooches to sleep under. This was done by snapping two ponchos together to form a small tent then using a third poncho as a ground cloth. While one of us pulled guard, the other two could sleep. These three-man positions were our standard way of operating most of the time. When it rained, we could catch rainwater off the ponchos to drink, saving us having to carry so much. The ground cloth separated us from a lot of the insects and crawlies that occupied the jungle floor. It wasn't uncommon to roll up the ground cover in the morning to find some creatures had spent the night under it sharing the dry spot and our body heat. Bamboo vipers liked to do this as did centipedes and a whole variety of other insects. We slept fully clothed with our boots on. The last thing you needed was to go running through the jungle barefooted should we be hit or have to move in the middle of the night. Most nights I would remove my boots, clean my feet wiping them with a sweat rag then put them back on.

This one night I got a bug in my ear. I was going to have last watch, I had just settled in to sleep when I was awakened by something crawling in my ear. I wanted to scream and run around. I was sure one giant centipede was about to feast on my brain. By digging at it with my finger, it only retreated farther into my ear canal. By this time, I'm going mad trying to maintain noise discipline and get some help for my dilemma in the dark. We had separated into squads manning different positions along the ridgeline about a hundred yards apart. The platoon medic was with the next squad down the ridge. In order to get to him I would have to go out through our claymores and trip wires, then go through their trip wires and claymores in order to enter their perimeter. We got on the radio and talked it over with the LT and the medic. It was decided at first to be too dangerous, both for me and the possibility of giving away our position should I trip a flare. The medic said the bug would die in my ear canal from the wax if I could only wait it out. I tried to wait it out, but the bug wouldn't die, and it was as active as ever clawing and biting its way to my brain. I got back on the radio and warned the LT that I was headed for their position and not to fire me up. With my weapon and a couple of grenades, I began to feel my way down the ridge towards the medic. I followed a claymore wire out to a claymore and knew there would be a trip wire a few feet beyond that. I got down on my hands and knees feeling for the trip wire while trying to concentrate on the job at hand and ignoring the bug still chomping away at my brain stem. This was the easy part. The hard part would come when I came to their trip wires. It seemed to take forever to cross that ground. I followed a small animal trail that straddled the ridge and came to the trip wire that marked the edge of their perimeter. Calling in a low voice, I let them know I was on my way in. Once I was inside their defenses, the guys hustled me over to the doc's hole. He spread a poncho over the two of us so that he could use a light to look in my ear. After a few minutes the bug came to the light, and Doc grabbed him with a pair of forceps. He made some comment about how good a shape the bug was still in and that in all of his time as a medic he had never seen one last the way that one did. I was just glad to have the thing out of my ear. I spent the rest of the night at the Doc's position rejoining my squad the next morning. I packed up my ruck sack and got ready to move out with my squad.

Every day in the bush started out with a hump to get away from our NDP site. This was SOP to keep the enemy from having time to form up around us or to be able to bring mortars in on us.

Often when we would stop for that first break in the morning, we would get a chance to eat some C-rations while the flag was figuring out where we were going or what our mission was going to be for that day. Some days we would move all day as part of the mission. Other times we might move into an ambush site and spend the whole day waiting for Charley to walk into our trap. Often times we would hump to an LZ to be flown out to another place in the jungle and inserted into a new area. As individual soldiers we were seldom informed as to why or where we were going in the big scheme of things. Most of the places we went didn't have names. They had numbers like Hill 907 and a grid coordinate. The numbers were very forgettable, but the sights and sounds and smells, the things that happened there were not. This one time we were to fly into an LZ on the side of a mountain. The first bird in always had a radio man on board, and today that would be me. I had the radio for our squad leader, Sergeant Berry. Our job was to secure the LZ for the rest of the birds coming in behind us and to keep them informed of conditions on the ground as they were landing.

It was a beautiful morning to be sitting in the door of a Huey. I was behind the co-pilot on the right side looking at the rest of the flight behind us and the cobra gunships escorting us to our destination. I could see the LZ ahead and the artillery rounds impacting there being fired from a firebase miles away. My mind was churning as I caught the eyes of the other grunts. All of us were lost in our own thoughts and preparations for what awaited us on the ground. The cobras were right alongside us now. I could see the rockets leaving their pods to fly and strike the LZ. The artillery barrage lifted as we drew closer, and the cobras peeled off to circle the area. The door gunners opened up with their M-60s as we came floating down to the LZ. We had to jump off and run to the sides in order to clear the blades as the pilot turned his bird and headed down hill to get airborne. We ran to the side and then up the hill to a place where we could have a good view of the LZ. By the time this was accomplished, two more birds had dropped their loads. Sergeant Berry told me to inform the rest of the flight that the LZ was booby-trapped and sent a man down to wave off the next helicopter. I got on the horn to the flight, and they were rerouted to loiter until further notice. The guy who went to wave off the next bird was brand new. As he approached the incoming bird from the uphill side, there was a sound from the rooter as it struck him. For a second the world went silent. That sound permeated everything. Every man on the ground knew instantly what had happened. The bird discharged its load and turned away downhill, the wind from the blades exposing the claymores hidden in the trees. Why none of them went off, I'll never know. They had made it through the artillery prep, machine gun fire and four helicopters coming in. We went to work to clear the LZ, blowing the trees down with C-4 that held the claymores. In the time since our landing the sun had begun to beat down. The body under its poncho and the blood around it mixed with the smell of the artillery, the C-4, the gun powder, and the jungle. We set to work to get the rest of the birds in until our whole company was on the ground. The new guy rolled in his poncho was loaded on the last bird in. There were trails all over the ridgeline we had landed on and signs of enemy activity everywhere. We were a full company and spoiling for a fight, but we were not to get it. What we were to get was the slow burning lesson, that Charley had been there before us.

He had prepared for us a reception of his choosing, and even though his plan wasn't foolproof, we had blundered and cost us a man. There was one other casualty that day, my little Olympus Penn camera. I had left it sitting on my rucksack when we pulled back to blow a tree down. When the tree came down, it struck my camera smashing it. The next several days were spent patrolling and ambushing in that area. Our point men found a number of booby-traps, but we were unable to close with the enemy.

BACK ON BIRMINGHAM

We were airlifted on to Fire Support Base Birmingham. The company arrived there late in the afternoon. While we were getting settled in to our bunker assignments, we could smell chow being served. We were told that we could have two beers or cold sodas each, but that we were too late for hot chow. We would just have to be satisfied with C-rations for another day. For the last three weeks we had been humping the bush on C-rations and bomb crater water. Three of the guys from our squad went to the mess hall anyway and spoke to the mess cooks, asking if there were any leftovers. The cooks defended their prerogative to stop serving at a given time regardless of when the infantry decided to show up. There were seven or eight mess cooks, but the three grunts weren't backing down. They put up one hell of an argument comparing their job in the bush to that of a mess cook and calling into question the genetic heritage required in the formation of mess cooks in general. Somehow while all this was going on a case of beef roasts disappeared from a freezer in the back of the mess tent. We had a small fire going being fed by ammo crates and mortar boxes. We borrowed a metal folding chair from somewhere up near the TOC. Once we had the paint burned off, that chair made a serviceable grill. Arne used his machete to slice steaks off the rolled roasts. Over the next couple of hours that beef went into the bellies of the grunts on Birmingham. That night some of us sat up late watching that fire die down and talking.

John was on his third tour in Nam. What he and the more experienced grunts had to say carried a lot of weight with us. Recently we had been hearing about the Vietnamization of the war. The US was planning to reduce the size of its forces handing the fighting over to the South Vietnamese Military. John and some of the others were of the opinion that the ARVN didn't as a whole have the will to sustain the fight with the north. John asked how many of us had received Dear John letters from our girlfriends. Most of the guys acknowledged that they had. He went on to say that US soldiers were so unpopular in the states that they were being spit on at the airports and that the wives and girlfriends faced a lot of social pressure for their association, especially with Vietnam veterans. While we were over here, the world back home was changing radically. The blacks were standing up for their rights. Women were standing for more rights, and there was both a sexual and social revolution going on. There were fewer of us around the fire now, perhaps ten of us. The only one not from our platoon was a guy known to me as Clyde the sniper.

Clyde was with L company rangers. They kept a couple of sniper teams at work off of Birmingham. Clyde and I had hit it off after spending some time in the OP together trading life stories while scanning the landscape for troop movement. Clyde was twenty-five when he received his induction notice. He had graduated with a degree in psychology and was just starting to practice when the army intervened offering him a chance to be an officer and a gentleman if he would sign for another year. Clyde refused the offer, and as a result, the army discovered his talent for placing rounds in tight groups at extreme ranges. Clyde had never fired a weapon before entering the military. He was from Salt Lake, nearly bald and as mild-mannered and soft-spoken a man as I could ever hope to meet. At 25 Clyde was the oldest of any of us there around that camp fire. He had a number of confirmed kills as confided to me not by him but by his team mates. He was such an enigma, this most lethal of one-shot tacticians in the body of a short, balding, academic of Brigham Young. Another foible of the Vietnam experience was that nothing ever was as it seemed.

That night under a clear sky we gorged on stolen steaks and listened to one another as the firelight played on our faces. Sergeant Berry spoke of his first two days in the platoon, carrying bodies off a hill at the edge of the Asha Valley. Scotty and John were there at that fight but would rather talk about R&R in Bangkok. In the rounds of talk there were subjects sacred, like going home. Most of that talk was reserved for the shorties, the two-digit midgets, those with less than one hundred days left in country. They could expound with some confidence about the lives they would lead after the army. For the rest of us, it was taboo. With hundreds of days left to serve, our offerings were just the chirping of birds, pleasant to listen to but with no meaning.

Clyde spoke about the effects of the combat experience on individuals and the war in general and its effects on the society we would be going back to. His ability to boil things down to make them understandable to us was remarkable. We have a mission to fulfill for the army every day. That is to seek out and kill the enemy at every opportunity. To carry out that mission we must close ourselves off from what the politicians are saying about the shape of the negotiating table where they will sit to debate the fate of this landscape. We must ignore the protests about black and white and sexual rights. We can't be distracted by the hippy that is dating our girlfriend or the latest celebrity that is protesting the war. Our job here is to survive this tour.

The very act of having these conversations was counter to jungle survival. The moment we stepped outside the wire we were in Charlie's backyard. In order to play the game on his level, you had to be uncompromised by all the distractions. Those who had been in country for a while cautioned us to never allow ourselves to be captured. Better to die trying to escape rather than to be taken alive. It had come down to them from others who had been through it what a captured grunt could expect. The NVA had no prison space for line soldiers. If captured alive, we could expect to be executed on the spot or paraded through a camp or village where we would be beaten to death with sticks and stones by the residents. Even the gentlest spirit when forced to bash the brains out of a bound captive, will then spend the rest of their lives trying to justify it. By doing so, the NVA gained a psychological convert and rid themselves of the bother and expense of a prisoner of no military value.

We broke it up and went our separate ways at first light. There were no showers available for us, so the company set up security at the river, and we all got a chance to bathe. When they saw we had a bathing area secure, people from other units came to take advantage of a chance to get into the river safely. A Charlie model helicopter came and landed in the shallows next to a duce and half. Their crews were happy joining us for a swim and the chance to wash their vehicles.

Ten minutes after our swim we were dry and hot, and a new layer of dust was sticking to our sweat. My squad would be outside of the wire that night, so we had the rest of the day off to sleep, eat and play cards. Sergeant Berry led nine of us out through the wire just at dusk. Our destination was the gravel point, a place between the river and the fire base where the engineers had set up a gravel processing plant. The gravel was used to maintain the roads in the area. The engineers had some problems with booby traps being set around their work area, so our intention was to prevent that happening again and to act as a listening post for infiltration from the river and the road that led to the west. After a hump of about thirty minutes, we settled into a spot that gave us a view of the road, the gravel point, and the river. The terrain was fairly open sloping away toward the river with some brush about six feet high that we concealed ourselves in. By the rising moon we set out our claymores and established our fields of fire. We had only been in position for a few minutes when we heard steps coming from the west at an even pace. Bugs had his M-60 trained on the road toward the coming sound. Four claymore clickers with safeties off were ready to go. Eight M-16s and an M-79 grenade launcher were trained on the road each with a GI with his safety off and pressure on the trigger. The sound of the marching came closer and closer to the bend in the road and the entrance to our kill zone. By the thinnest of margins, we held ourselves in check as the marching feet came into view in the moonlight. None of us fired on the water buffalo. He must have sensed us waiting there poised to kill. He slowed his pace and wandered to the opposite side of the road from us sniffing the air and cropping a little grass. I could hear the safeties click back on, and a couple of guys quietly clear their throats as the big animal slowly browsed his way through our ambush site. He stuck around for what seemed like several hours but was probably perhaps ten minutes. Then he resumed his pace towards the East and his hoof falls steadily dissipated after we had lost sight of him.

What had moments before caused our adrenalin to spike now was gone in the moonlight leaving us to get our nerves back under control and be prepared for the real thing. No doubt the water buffalo had been used by the NVA to move goods somewhere out along the border. He had likely belonged to some farmer and had been commandeered for that use. When he got loose, he headed home like livestock tend to do. It would have been against the best interest of our mission to give away our position. Had we been out on patrol and run across an unattended buffalo, our orders would have been to destroy him. I remained awake for the rest of the night along with several of the others who were still relatively new in country. The guys who had been here longer took it in stride and were able to crash letting us spend the rest of the night staring at the shadows cast by the moonlight and listening for sounds that didn't belong.

At dawn we radioed the TOC that we were coming in and to inform those on watch along the bunker line not to fire us up. After reentering the wire, we dropped our gear and headed for the mess tent. The company clerk was there and informed us that today was pay day and that we could come up to the TOC throughout the day to get our pay. Our squad leaders would let us know when we were to report for pay. Payday was always a little bit of a lighter day if we were not under attack or out in the bush sneaking around. Very few of us took all of our pay, most guys had an allotment taken out that went home or to a spouse. Whatever cash we had coming after that was paid in MPC (military payment certificates). It looked like and was about the size of Monopoly Money. The military issued it to help control the black-market trade. They would recall it and change the denominations every six months or so to keep large amounts of money from concentrating in the wrong hands. Just about everyone had at least some money on payday and that is when the poker games would kick off. We had in our squad a pretty fair player name Kit. Kit was from Indiana and had a girlfriend/fiancé that went to Kent State. Kit was a real mellow guy. The only aggressive moves I ever saw him make were at the poker games that broke out on payday. He was intimately familiar with every form of poker I had ever heard of and some new variations besides. Most of our platoon had received their pay by early afternoon, each of us receiving our funny money and signing for it. Uncle Sam wanted the books to balance even when we had no place to go and nowhere to spend it.

The poker game broke out in bunker nine well before dark. Kit had a fresh deck of cards and was doing most of the dealing. Ponchos were hung over the entrances to the bunker to keep the candle light from giving away its position. I finished up first watch that night at bunker twelve and arrived at the game just before midnight. The guys welcomed me in offering me a warm Schlitz and a seat in the game. Mail had reached us and had been delivered to us just before evening chow. I was feeling light after a couple of letters from home. Several of the guys in the game had already been at it for five or six hours including Kit. After dealing a few hands of stud, Kit sat out to read his mail. I dealt a couple of hands and was a little ahead when our attention was drawn to Kit. His face was red, and he looked like he was about to cry. Angry words squeezed between his teeth about a shooting at Kent State where some idiot had fired up a student. I won several good-sized pots as we played on and called for Kit to read us the letters. There were two of them from his girl. The first one spoke of the shootings that had occurred on the campus. Kit's girl had been there and had heard the shots. Some of us commented that the National Guardsmen must not have had good fire discipline otherwise they would have got more of the worthless demonstrators. Clyde chimed in, "No, this is bad. Dead civilians, especially American students, are going to reflect poorly on all service men." John replied that it was only four students, that is less than we lose over here on the average half day. Clyde's reply was that the news media loves the poor students, even the demonstrators, while they hate our guts and will go out of their way to portray us as heartless killers like Caley at May Li.

Gosh, I can't believe my luck! I've won another nice pot. "Hey, Kit, what does the other letter say?" As he read from the other letter the place got quiet. She was devastated by the shootings at her school and in the light of such a tragedy she could no longer continue to correspond with someone involved in the Vietnam

War. Then there was something about what to do with the ring he had given her and have a nice life. We all felt bad. Not just for Kit but for ourselves because we all knew we had it coming. Not because we deserved it. But because the draft dodging crowd at home were the darlings of the media, and their point of view was the only one that was going to see the light of day.

With Kit out of the game, I won pot after pot. I went to chow that morning with an ammo can full of MPC. There was over fifteen hundred dollars in that can. After breakfast the spell was broken, I managed to lose all but about four hundred dollars of the money.

The old timers welcomed Kit to the club telling the rest of us it was just a matter of time until our Dear Johns arrived. They were prompt to remind us that Charley loved the protesters and Walter Cronkite and were waiting for us just outside the wire.

REMEMBER BILLY

Remember Billy from AIT? Well, I saw him in Vietnam. Mike Corral and I (we were the procurement team) were hitchhiking from Pho Bai to fire base Birmingham. A convoy went by us and the last vehicle in the convoy was an MP Duck. It pulled over to give us a ride. When I reached up to grab the hand that was held down to me, it was Billy. We locked eyes and remembered each other immediately. It went through my mind, "Does he remember who I was and was he still pissed?" Two of the guys on the duck were black, so he had obviously made changes in his life outlook. Within a few minutes we were all swapping stories about our experiences. Within a few minutes, Ol' Billy offered to smoke a joint with me, apparently our differences had been reconciled.

CLYDE THE SNIPER

Clyde the Sniper was very unpretentious. You never heard him brag about his abilities or those of his unit. We had been trained since basic that the unit we were in was the best and to take great pride in who we were. No doubt it is a fine motivational tool to get everyone believing they are the best, and I had the privilege to serve with some damn fine people. As draftees, we were considered inferior to those who volunteered. Being a draftee infantryman in Vietnam was the worst job in the army. In that, though, was our power. Nobody wanted our job. What could they do to us? If we were busted, they had to make us a PFC before they could send us back to the field. The difference in pay grade from PFC to spec-4 was only 30 dollars a month. As a result, we didn't think we were bad; we knew we were bad. We were the ones that went outside the wire. Anybody could join our club. All you had to do was survive long enough to be recognized as a member. When it was time to board the helicopters for the next mission, who was going to be there? The ones that came back time after time developed a kind of gravity. They had the knack for survival, and they were drawn to one another. These were the guys who did the real work of the infantry.

Our squad was picked for a mission up on a mountain called Nui Que. We would be inserted onto the top of the hill and establish radio contact with a unit down in the canyon on the other side. They needed us to relay their traffic to the rear in order to maintain communications. Nui Que had been fought over many times over the years. The top of it was solid rock. We were told that its elevation had been reduced by thirty feet after the battle ship New Jersey had worked it over several years prior to our being there. One bird at a time could land on its flat top. I was on the first bird in. Twelve of us made up the group for the mission. We quickly set up four fighting positions with excellent fields of fire down the sides of the barren rock. I got my long john up and established communications with the TOC and the unit we were there to support. I plotted and called for a round of white phosphorus 200 up to inform the artillery where we might need fire should the NVA challenge our position. By the time Sergeant Berry had checked the fighting positions, we had eaten some C-rations. It was getting dark.

The night was clear, and you could see for miles from the top of the hill. Up at Camp Sally and over to Phu Bai and Hue City there were lights that illuminated the American and South Vietnamese held positions. More lights like jewels on velvet dotted the South China Sea to the east. Boats were out fishing. Our navy and those of our allies swept the waters monitoring ocean traffic. To the west was total darkness with occasional illumination popping up out of the jungle or a line of tracers reaching towards a black place in the landscape. Out along the border where the Ho Chi Min trail ran down from the north, B-52s were dropping their ordinance. The horizon there lit up red and orange as their bombs sought out prey. The sound was like a coffee percolator and lent a sense of security that our guys were out in the night bringing hell to Charley keeping us safe for now. From here I could hear the guns fire from Birmingham and Arsenal and listen for the report of the warheads as they impacted at their targets. When a target was out beyond us and in line with the source of fire, you could hear and in daylight see the rounds as they passed over head. They made a sound peculiar to themselves, a little like a train going by.

The company we were relaying for started to have an increase in radio traffic at about four in the morning, just before dawn. Their perimeter was being probed on three sides, and it looked like they were being tested by a large force of NVA. I was on the horn continuously relaying their position to TOC, artillery and ARA. Because of their position deep in the canyon below us, artillery could not be effectively brought to bear. They were, however, able to bring rounds in on avenues of approach and to provide illumination over their position. Just as the sun came up, the firing in the canyon increased. From our position on the hill we could hear M-16 and M-60 mixing it up with AK, hand grenades and M-79. Requests were sent in for gunships as the battle below us heated up. Ammunition resupply was called for and was inbound. When the resupply bird arrived at their position, it was unable to land or discharge the resupply because of fog in the canyon. We were above the fog, so their resupply was offloaded at our location until the weather cleared, and a bird could make it back to complete the resupply. Along with the resupply, came one replacement. He was a new guy fresh out of training on his first trip to the field. Sergeant Berry put him in a position watching down the hill just a few feet from where I had my radio set up. I had a voice box on the radio, so I could move around a bit and still monitor the traffic. The radio traffic that was coming from our sister company down the hill was being broadcast from my radio, and the new guy could hear it. A fire fight had been going off and on all morning. By now there were several casualties. As we sat there, we could hear the exchange of gun fire in the distance. Over the voice box came the calls for medivac, resupply and air support. None of this could be accomplished due to the lack of visibility at the engaged company's location. During a lull in the radio traffic, I went over the replacement's gear with him explaining to him that he would be dropped into a hot LZ and that he should be ready to engage the enemy as soon as he hit the ground. While I was explaining this to him, in the background was the voice box with the LT pleading for support and the cries of his wounded behind him whenever his mike was keyed. I could see the fear mounting in the eyes of the newbie and tried to reassure him that as soon as the fog began to lift there would be gunships, medical evacuation and resupply on the way. It was the same message I had been delivering to the embattled company all morning. I left the replacement's position telling him to check his magazines again and put the best ones where he would need them first. I went back to my radio and began to relay more traffic for the company in the canyon. The fog was lifting, and they wanted the gun ships in to help clear their perimeter and allow a medical evacuation helicopter in to remove their wounded. In the background was the sounds of the firefight, and the sound of men screaming to each other across the contested ground.

A single shot cut short by immediate impact brought everyone in our little perimeter to the ground. There was a moment of confusion when each of us searched our fields of fire for hostile targets.

The new replacement had been hit. His left boot was turning red as he laid aside his M-16. It took all of us a few seconds to grasp what had taken place. There was a look of shock and fear on the guy's face as the realization of what he had done to himself took hold of him. "You dumb, slime-ball newbie, coward, idiot! Now look what you've done!" is what Sergeant Berry said to break the silence. "Your unit is down there needing your help, and your first move is to shoot the end of your foot off!" It took a good ten minutes for all of us to fire our first salvo of insults at this goof ball. I told him I wouldn't call for a medivac and that he could bleed out for all I cared, fresh meat piece of dung. He was in shock by then. The real pain hadn't set in yet.

Gun ships were on station, and I got occupied with relaying radio traffic between them and our brothers down in the fight. Several of the guys went to work on the replacement. Getting his boot off was a major hurtle. It looked like he would lose all but his big toe. They got a couple of battle dressings on the place where his toes used to be and gave him a shot of morphine to shut him up. He laid on his back with his foot elevated while the resupply bird came in to pick up the goods going out to his unit. The resupply bird came back by on its way out to evacuate the newbie. Four of the guys dumped him unceremoniously onto the deck of the resupply bird. The pilot pulled pitch and that is the last we ever saw or heard of him. The bloody boot laid there near the fighting position that the newbie had occupied for less than a day. We speculated that he was on a hospital ship in the South China Sea getting fussed over by a pretty young nurse while he entertained her with the story of how he won his purple heart, a tale of gritty combat and courage under fire.

Our job was to hold down our place on the hill and to keep communications open to the company that was beyond the reach of direct radio traffic. We remained there two more days as the enemy was driven back in the canyon below. We relayed the message on the second day that the company was being pulled out and to be prepared for extraction just after first light. After their air lift was complete, two birds came back for us. I was on the last bird off of Nui Que that day. As we lifted off, the boot was still there, a little testament to our stay.

Back on Birmingham over a beer with Clyde, we were having a good time at the expense of the newbie. Some who weren't there on the mountain were full of ideas about what we should have done to him. It was Clyde's opinion that every man has his breaking point and that this guy's was pretty low. He said all of us could break. It was just a matter of time and circumstance. Several of the guys with more time in country mumbled a halfhearted agreement. Some guys just break. It's never pretty, but if it is going to happen, better get it over with early, less collateral damage that way. John related that on his second tour a guy in his squad, who was a solid soldier with six months in country and a number of contacts behind him, just stood up during a fire fight. He stood up and looked around like he was lost. He took three rounds center mass, didn't last long enough to see a medivac. The feeling in his squad was that the guy just broke.

In the hours and days spent silently guarding a position or humping through the boonies, my mind turned over every possible way that I might react under fire. I prayed that I could function properly when my time came. One of the new guys asked, "What was the guy's name?" None of us knew. We got several answers back. "It's the same as yours, Fresh Meat Newbie." We all wanted to do our jobs well, and we all wanted to survive. I talked to the Doc about my feet. He gave me some foot powder and told me to let the sun shine on them as much as I could to dry them out. The soles of my feet looked like the craters on the moon.

Our next mission would take us to the field as a company. We assembled on the chopper pad below Birmingham and waited for our lift to take us out. Twenty Hueys with six troops each lifted off the pad. Our bird was near the center of the flight as we trailed in line to the north and east. We were inserted unopposed in an area of low rolling hills. As we exited the birds into the storm of dust kicked up by the rotors, the heat and humidity greeted us and made the weight of our rucksacks increase. Once the whole company was on the ground each platoon went off in different directions to look for signs of enemy activity. The flag, (that is the company commander), was with another platoon. Our platoon leader was LT Whalen. He was a big easy-going guy who did his best to keep us in line while fulfilling the requirements of the mission. Intelligence had information that indicated that the enemy was caching weapons and equipment in this area. We were to find them and engage the enemy should we find him. Each day we would hump to a new hill and set up as a platoon, then move off as squads to search the surrounding area for signs of enemy activity. On our fourth day in the bush we were resupplied. Bugs, our machine gunner, needed a new bolt for his M-60. His had broken the first day in the field, and a replacement had not come out with the load. After receiving our resupply, we moved away from the LZ and continued the mission. A new standing order had come down that we were all to wear our steel pots at all times in the bush. Most of us liked to wear a bush hat, dawning the steel pot only when we felt like we were about to make contact. Some guys got rid of their helmets all together. The morning after resupply, we were given a new area to search. It was about three miles to the new AO, so we were trying to get most of it behind us before it got too hot. Going down into some thick brush between two hills, we ran across some old trails where we spent several hours looking for sign. Nothing came of it but more heat and exhaustion. We came up out of there at about 1300 hours and continued to hump our rucks in the direction of our new AO. By this time, it was really hot, and we were moving across open ground. A helicopter flew over, then circled and landed on our direction of march. Some brass stepped out of the bird with his entourage in tow and proceeded to talk to the LT. From where I sat against my rucksack, I could see what was going on. The Colonel and the First Sergeant were working their way along the line giving a lecture to anyone who didn't have a helmet on. LT Whalen followed taking the names down of those who were noncompliant. Bugs was just in front of me helmetless in the line of march. When the colonel began to lecture Bugs, all hell broke loose. Bugs threw his M-60 to the ground at the colonel's feet saying, "You rotten, SOB, you have come out here to fine me for not having a helmet? You want to lecture me over not having a helmet? I'm packing twenty-seven pounds of machinegun and can't get your REMFs to send me out a bolt to make it fire. I'm supposed to engage the enemy with a twenty-seven-pound club, and you want to give me hell about a helmet. Well ---- you and---- the army." John and I and several others got close enough to Bugs to restrain him should he need it. His tirade continued on while the colonel and his first sergeant got back into his bird and lifted off. Bugs was always such a quiet guy; the colonel's visit must have caught him at the wrong time. About an hour later just as we were reaching our new AO that same helicopter returned minus the colonel but with a brand-new M-60 machinegun. The pilot and the rest of the crew were grinning from ear to ear as they pulled pitch to get out of there. Bugs had spoken for all of us who were out doing the job no one else wanted. The colonel must have been a man of some understanding. Although we all were in fear of some reprisal, none ever came. As it turned out, I began to wear my helmet nearly all of the time after experiencing some rocket and mortar attacks and seeing some head wounds. I came to learn that there were times when I wished that I could get my whole body into my helmet, and the realization that I couldn't wasn't for lack of trying.

Every three to four months we would take part in a battalion stand down. It would take place over a week. We were flown in to our rear area at Phu Bai where we were treated to hot showers and mess hall food, clean jungle fatigues and cold beer at the EM (Enlisted Men's) club. It was also a chance to go to the dentist or doctor. This all took place between classes on the latest booby traps that the enemy was deploying in our area and refresher classes in such things as first aid, stream crossing, repelling and sexually transmitted diseases. We would also go to the range and zero our weapons and see the guys at the armory about any problems with our equipment. The week would wind up with two days at Eagle Beach, the stand down area of the 101st at Tan My Island on the South China Sea. There was always a party atmosphere at stand down compared to humping the boonies or providing security at one of the fire bases. There were cots for us to sleep on inside of screened in hooches. These were luxury accommodations for a bunch of line dogs.

On the second day of stand down our platoon was to practice stream crossings. We marched with our rucksacks and gear to a pond nearby where the class would take place. Two rangers were our instructors and began by showing us how to wrap our rucksacks and gear in our ponchos in such a way as to allow us to swim with it as a flotation device. We were paired up into teams of two for the exercise. My teammate for the exercise was a new recruit who had just been with the platoon for a week. He was a black guy from Illinois who became known as Brother Walker. He had a great sense of humor, was always up for a laugh and still had the newbie habit of trying to make friends with everyone. We watched as the guys before us threw their flotation devices into the water then swam out to them in full uniform to retrieve them and swim with them back to shore. When it came to our turn to test our device, the Rangers threw our rucksack wrapped in our ponchos out into the middle of the pond which had become a murky mud hole from all of the activity we had subjected it to. I dove in first and surfaced near our flotation device. I swam a few feet to it and held on waiting for Brother Walker to follow. Brother Walker executed a running dive towards my location surfacing about ten feet away. Somewhere between entering the water and surfacing the look on Brother Walker's face went from one of supreme confidence to abject terror. His eyes locked on mine as I waved him on towards the flotation device. He was flailing his arms in terrified dog paddle style that was barely keeping his head above water. The guys on shore were laughing and hooting thinking Brother Walker was putting on a show of drowning. I may have been the first to realize that he was in real trouble and started to push the flotation device in his direction. He was going down for the third time when two guys from the shore and I all reached him at the same time. We got him to shore clinging to the flotation device which by now was nearly waterlogged. Several pairs of hands drug him up the bank where he spit and coughed up a couple of quarts of water. The two rangers in charge of the class used the incident as a teaching tool to reinforce the importance of stream crossing skills. Brother Walker was his old self in a few minutes making jokes about his dive and thinking that if he entered the water with enough momentum, he could surface next to the flotation device, and no one would know that he could not swim.

We all learned some things from Brother Walker that day. Number one was how much we all depended on each other. What stronger demonstration of that could there be than his willingness to dive into that mud hole, and when his plan failed, we would be there to back him up. Of course, that didn't stop us from calling him The Dolphin for the rest of stand down or referring to Flipper being his favorite TV show.

Demetri came into the platoon as a replacement at the same time as Brother Walker. Demetri was from the Ukraine over in Russia. He got a job on a ship hauling iron ore to Canada. He jumped ship there and crossed the border into the United States. When things started to go wrong for him in the States, he volunteered for the draft in order to become a citizen. Guess he figured it was a bargain compared with life in the Soviet Union. A couple of days after Brother Walker and Demetri joined our squad, Demetri came to Sergeant Berry with a complaint. "We in Ukraine don't have no black people. I cannot be around dis guy so much." Sergeant Berry had put the two of them together on the gun team and made it clear to them that they would have to work out whatever differences they had. His last word on the subject was, "If you can't get along, get it on." Brother Walker said something like, "You crazy, toothless, Russian honky you come on, and I'll stomp the Ukrainian crap out of you." Demetri put on a bold face stepping forward and exchanging a few punches with Brother Walker, but he didn't have the kind of heart to sustain his bigotry. Brother Walker won by unanimous decision. The two of them became a solid pair for the gun team. But Brother Walker never quit calling him Honky Ukraine and Demetri referred to him as Dat' Black Guy. Either one of them would have taken a bullet for the other.

Our last two days of stand down were spent at Eagle Beach. While there, we had no duties whatsoever. The bar was open from ten in the morning till long past midnight. The mess hall was serving three meals a day, and the beach never closed. There was a USO show that played twice a day in the club. They were a band from Korea that cranked out top forty hits from the sixties with an Asian accent. We sang and laughed at the band and at ourselves and nursed every drop of pleasure out of that time knowing we were headed back to the bush tomorrow. The next morning, we shouldered our rucksacks and boarded the LCT that served as a ferry between Tan My and the mainland. There we were met by two cattle trucks that hauled us back to Phu Bai through the ancient capital of Hue. As we rode in the open trucks, we looked out on the rivers and canals that that served as roads through the old city and saw the sites where so much fighting had taken place two years before during the Tet offensive of 1968. The city was bustling with bicycle and moped traffic along with water buffalo carts and every ancient kind of conveyance imaginable. As the trucks slowed going through the down town, hawkers yelled and held up their wares. The boom-boom girls called from their balconies, "You numba-one GI. I love you too much." Guys yelled back, "I love you too, Babe San," all the while clutching their weapons and searching the crowds for the person with a grenade to toss among us. Cowoys on motorcycles streamed past the trucks stripping the wrist watches off of any wrist within reach of the rider on the back. Cowoy is a Vietnamese word meaning thief. Of course, GI's made it into "cowboy", and called any young male below military age "cowboy" to which they would reply, "Me no cowoy." Most GIs weren't aware of this, so the misunderstanding stood between us, and I'm sure contributed to a lot of miscommunication between the general population and US military personnel. Nobody likes their sons and grandsons to be referred to as thieves, even when they are.

We untrucked in the company area at Phu Bai later that afternoon. We would have one more night to sleep on a cot before returning to the bush. With new and repaired gear and fresh ammo we were on the chopper pad at 0800 eating C-rations for breakfast and waiting on an airlift to take us out to the field. Our platoon was inserted onto a knoll in the foothills west of FSB Birmingham. From there we moved further west into the mountains and heavy jungle terrain. Our mission was to locate enemy equipment caches that the intelligence guys said were in the area. We were finding plenty of booby-traps and enemy sign, but after three days had not made contact or found anything more than unoccupied camps and a small amount of rice. The next day a dog handler would be sent out to aid us in the search. We figured they must be hiding their stuff in caves or burying it to be retrieved at some time in the future.

The following day found us in triple canopy jungle when a message came in over the radio that the dog and his handler were inbound to our location. We began to search for a place where there was a hole in the canopy large enough for them to repel down to us. We located a spot with about a twenty-foot hole through the first two layers of canopy and no tall trees so that a helicopter could hover at about one hundred feet and drop the repel rope through the hole. The bird came up on our frequency, and we talked him into our location without much trouble. As he hovered over the hole, the dog came out first and was lowered to the jungle floor by his handler. Once the dog was on the ground, it was up to one of us to unhook him from the repel rope and keep him calm until he could be reunited with his partner. This dog sat quietly looking up through the trees for his master. Apparently, this wasn't his first mission. From where I sat with my radio, I had a pretty good partial view of the helicopter and the dog handler as he stood on the skid of the Huey getting ready to repel down. Around the hole was a matrix of vine bamboo like a spider's web growing through trees and brush that grew to a height of about forty feet. The handler kicked away from the skid and was just beginning his decent when the repel rope burned through his Swiss seat. He was loaded down with all of his gear for him and the dog. As the rope making up his harness unwrapped, he was twisted around upside down and spun several times. The crew chief must have yelled something to the pilot because just before he was separated completely from the repel rope the helicopter shifted sideways just enough so that the handler was thrown to the side of the hole. He fell the first fifty feet rucksack first upside down. Crashing through the branches of the taller trees, he was caught by the web of vine bamboo and hung suspended about twenty feet off of the ground. His dog became highly agitated and bit the guy who was holding him attaining his release. He ran to where he had a better view of proceedings and growled his displeasure at the way we were doing things. Two of the guys with machetes began to cut away brush to allow the handler to sink toward the ground. He was able to talk and let us know that he was ok, just so tangled in vines and rope and hanging upside down that he couldn't free himself. Four troopers got under him and held him up as the last branches were cut away that held him off the ground. In the midst of this, his dog was nipping at anyone he thought was trying to hurt his master. Before he was completely freed from the brush pile that saved him, he had to calm down the dog that was licking him and dancing his reunion dance. Once the handler was freed from all entanglements and we were sure he was ok, the bird that brought them in left the area and all was quiet once again. We were all happy that the handler was safe on the ground with us, and we had a good laugh about it. Five guys got bit by the dog in the ten minutes or so that it took the whole thing to come down. Most of us carried tetracycline for cuts and scratches, and the handler assured us that the dog had all his shots. Now our job was to get out of the area where we had raised such a ruckus.

Our point team kept up a pretty good pace for several hours before calling the dog team up front. The dog went on alert soon after being placed at the front of the column. In the next several hours he found two spider holes. A spider hole is a concealed fox hole near the trail where a trail watcher can monitor traffic on the trail to report our movement or he might have a command-detonated explosive device that he controls from that location.

We set up a hasty perimeter and ate C-rations before sun down. It was nice to have the dog with us. He and his handler had already proven their worth. We likely would not have found the spider holes without them. It was very clear that this dog was not for us to pet. He had a job to do, and he would answer to just one man for all of his human interaction. The bond between them was something that we all admired.

We were up and moving at day break. It was hot, damp, and dark under the canopy. The point kept a cautious pace as we moved forward uphill. Our squad was walking rear security when a break was called. As we took our positions, word came over the radio to bring the dog up to the front of the column. After the short water break, we were on the move again. When the platoon starts out, it's kind of like a caterpillar. The point stretches out as the middle and the end get the right interval of movement. Rear security had just hoisted our rucksacks and taken a few steps when an M-16 fired a short burst with the sound coming from up near the front of the column. We instantly hit the ground and looked for defensive positions. As it turned out, the point had become suspicious and called for the dog team to come up front. The dog instantly went on alert lunging at his leash. Just a couple of feet off the trail there was an NVA concealed in a spider hole. When the dog and handler came within reach of him, the dog tore into the spider hole and drug out the trail watcher. The trail watcher started to bring his AK to bear when the point man fired him up from about ten feet away. Our point man said that the dog never hesitated. He was on the guy in the spider hole and had hold of him before anyone had time to think about a prisoner or gathering intelligence.

It was an action like most of the actions I would experience during my tour. The actual fighting happened within a few yards of me, yet I didn't see the enemy till it was over. The body was searched for information, and the contact was radioed in to the TOC. We filed past the fallen enemy at the edge of the trail a few feet from his spider hole. The air under the jungle had taken on the metallic smell of fresh blood along with gasses escaping the body and burnt gun powder. We exited the area cautiously moving toward our next contact, away from the guy who had been surprised in his spider hole by a sniffer dog and a platoon of grunts. Someone had placed a cigarette butt between his lips and put a 101st Airborne patch over one eye. Our squad was walking rear security.

I kept a little tab running in the back of my head. How many did they give up for each one of ours? More useless information to try and fill the minutes and hours of tedium? What was it like to be that guy? To crouch for days in a spider hole gathering information on who was using the trail? Just a trail that connected to another and another all the way up to Hanoi and Uncle Ho. This guy had walked all the way down here from his home up north in order to make war on us. We came halfway around the world to see him.

Dog teams would generally stay out with us for no more than three days. My understanding was that after that the dogs need a break or they would work themselves to death. The team extracted on the bird that brought us our next resupply.

Monsoon season had begun turning life in the bush into a clinging quagmire of mud and leeches. The leeches kept near to the streams during the dry season, but when it got wet, they could be many yards from the streams. Every little puddle or step across could be full of them, and they would inhabit the grasses and low brush. They would hitch a ride as you passed by, then look for a way to get beneath your clothing. If you caught them before they could clamp on, you could just brush them off, but once they got their little teeth into you, you needed another method to dislodge them. If you just yanked them off, the teeth would stay in and you would get an infection. To make them release their grip you could hold a lit cigarette to them until they let go, giving you the satisfaction of burning the little buggers.

Squirting them with insect repellent was my method of choice. If you had one or more on your back someone else would have to assist in the de-leeching. You could not feel their bite they possessed a pain killer that desensitized it. Sometimes, they would hang there until they had their fill of your blood then die. In the morning you would find their swollen bodies about the size of your pinky finger full of your coagulated blood in the folds of your clothing. There is nothing to do then but pitch them out and put a drop of tetracycline on the bite mark.

Moving through the bush in the rain brought with it a whole different set of problems. Guys were constantly slipping and sliding in the muddy tracks left by those in front of him. One afternoon the platoon was moving uphill. My position was near the rear of the column as we moved through an opening where there was very little underbrush beneath tall teakwood trees. The front of the platoon was clawing their way up a steep portion of the hill while we waited for them to negotiate the muddy climb. LT Whalen was about half way up the worst part when Philip started up behind him by about twenty feet. Philip took two steps up the bank and slid back to the bottom falling right on his ass. When he went down, his M-79 grenade launcher discharged sending a high explosive round up the bank where it bounced off the ground hitting the LT square in the right butt cheek. All of us hit the ground as LT Whalen came sliding down the bank colliding in a muddy entanglement with Philip and the guy behind him. The point squad was on the radio wanting to know what had happened and someone from the TOC who was monitoring our freak wanted to know the same thing. I radioed back that it was a giant cluster centered round an accidental discharge and that I would get back to them when we sorted it out.

Doc was there helping to untangle the three man pile up and a break in place was called for while we could figure out the damage. LT Whalen had a huge bruise forming on his butt and upper right leg. Other than that, everyone was OK. The HE (high explosive) round for the M-79 has to travel twenty-seven feet before it arms itself. That is why it didn't explode on contact with the LT.

The TOC got back to us as we were moving out and wanted an update on our situation and to remind us how to properly carry and deploy the M-79. A mention was made about some kind of disciplinary action for Philip over the incident. Philip said, "Heck yes, send out a chopper to extract me from this mud bath and kick my sorry butt right out of the army. I deserve it."

We managed to get to the back of the ridge we were coming up and found a defendable position where we set up security, heated up some C's, and settled in for the night. We huddled under our ponchos and pulled our guard while staring into the pitch-black night, listening to the wind above the treetops. The rain fell in sheets and waves and sprinkles. It fell on the trees two hundred feet up, then dropped to the understory, then to the brush, then to the ground where it formed puddles and rivulets so that we were soaked from above and below. To pull a four-hour watch in that, staring with every nerve, trying to listen for any movement, windblown trees being knocked together, branches crashing to the forest floor, being responsible for those huddled in their ponchos trying to get a little sleep, seconds tick by like hours. At the end of four hours you are nearly deaf from noise and the strain of listening. You wake the guy who takes your place and crawl into the spot he vacates. It still holds a little of his body heat, and you fall into an exhausted sleep.

At dawn we were packing our gear in the rain getting ready to move out. I passed my cup of C-ration coffee around, and it came back to me with one last drink of mostly cold rainwater We were ready to move.

Doc took a look at the LT's butt, and it was blue, purple, and red from about eight inches from his upper thigh to halfway up his butt cheek. There were no choppers flying in this weather, so we spread most of the LT's load between us and moved out. I could see the pain on the LT's face as we started up the hill. We were all stiff and sore. A couple of hours of humping would warm us up and get a lot of the kinks out. I don't recall the LT ever giving Philip any guff about shooting him in the ass with an M-79. It was just one of those things. Another day in Nam!

We spent the next three days looking for Charley under the jungle in the rain. Our resupply couldn't make it out to us, so we went three more days without resupply. We were out of any kind of food and had carried on the mission for a fourth day on empty. Our point team guided us to a place at the top of a ridge where the canopy was only about a hundred feet deep. We set up our perimeter and built a fire to warm up and boil water. Our plan involved calling in the resupply to our location, then firing pop flares up through a hole in the canopy through the fog. If the resupply crew could see our flares, they could hover over the spot and bomb us with cases of C-rations. The plan worked, sort of. They dropped a case of C's for every man and even dropped our mail to us. We couldn't see the bird hovering over us, but we could hear them and communicate with them over the radio. As the cases of C-rations hit the jungle floor from over a hundred feet the boxes would disintegrate around the contents. Each of us sat next to an exploded box and ate as much as we could from the cans that had burst open. The unexploded cans were wiped clean and placed in our rucks. I had three cans that didn't explode and two more that had only tiny pin holes. I covered the pin holes with the piece of tape that comes on the bottom of a smoke grenade thinking that would keep the contents safe for a few days. The mood in the platoon was much improved with the food and mail. After gorging ourselves, we burned the C-ration boxes and moved away from the area along the ridge line. Over the next three days the rain never let up as we searched our assigned area for NVA. Or next resupply, again, could not get out to us. The platoon came together at noon to take a break and share whatever rations we had. I got together with my buddy, Mike Corral. He didn't have any C's left, so we heated up one of the cans I had put the tape on. It was C-ration spaghetti. The word was that a break in the weather was coming, so we would get resupply tomorrow. We had heard that pretty regularly lately, and it was wearing a little thin. After our noon break the platoon broke up into squads and assumed ambush sites along the ridge line.

Dark was falling, and it wasn't raining as we moved into our ambush site. The sun was setting turning the thin wisp of fog a shade of pink as the air began to clear, and the mosquitoes came out. Just as the last light of day fell, I began to have a terrible stomachache. Suddenly I was vomiting and had explosive diarrhea at the same time. Two of my squad mates drug me into the middle of the ambush site where they could watch over me without being close enough to get hit by what was being discharged. They returned to their positions leaving me there like a goat staked out to lure a tiger. I lay there in the dark with my pants down to my knees, crapping and throwing up until I was too exhausted to move or to battle the thousands of mosquitoes that had come to feast.

I broke at that moment thinking that if the enemy was to find me and kill me it would be an act of mercy. There was no way to do what I was doing quietly. In convulsing and thrashing around I was endangering my whole squad. I passed in and out of consciousness through the night. I vaguely remember waking up covered with dried body waste and mosquito bites and being loaded onto a helicopter. I have no memory of my first day and night in the evacuation hospital. When I came awake, Mike was in the cot next to me with an IV in his arm. He had suffered the same fate as me. We had food poisoning from the taped over cans. My case was further complicated by hookworm that I had contracted somewhere, so I had to take the cure for that as well. I was down from a hundred and forty to just over a hundred pounds. No wonder I was feeling so sluggish lately. Mike and I spent three days in the hospital then borrowed a jeep that was left unattended and drove to Hue City for a little unapproved leave. We met up with a couple of chopper pilots and spent the night barhopping our way through what the town had to offer. Mike and I dropped the pilots off at their company area, parked the jeep in another company's AO and made it back to our company area in time for morning chow. The company clerk saw us in the chow hall and told us we were reported AWOL. We would have to go before the captain when we caught up with him out in the field. There was a convoy going out to FSB Arsenal, and we were to join it for the ride out. Our convoy pulled on to Arsenal at about five in the afternoon. Our platoon was off the firebase on a mission, but Captain Arrington was on the base and expecting us in his command post after evening chow. Mike and I had been up for three days, hadn't showered or cleaned up in that time and were still reeking of booze when we went before the captain.

Captain Arrington was a good guy letting us off with an article fifteen and forfeiture of one week's pay for our detour to Hue City. He then gave us each a cigar and asked us what we thought of the new LT who had just taken over our platoon. We lit up our cigars and began to inform the captain. Mike opened up the discussion by saying that, if he slapped the LT in the face he would fall to his knees and cry like a baby.

On a previous mission we had been assigned to check out an area suspected of being a rocket launch site. Our squad was on point, and the new LT was with us. We came to an open spot on a ridge we had to go up about two hundred yards long. Our squad leader suggested we skirt around the open area in the brush, leaving half the squad there until the point could signal all clear from the top of the open spot. The LT said no, that we would just proceed across the opening. We argued that this was a perfect ambush site and that the NVA had the total advantage if they were waiting for us. We talked him into letting us move about halfway round the field and setting up so that we could offer covering fire for their approach across the field. The point team and our M-79 man along with me and my radio found a place where we could offer good covering fire to the right flank and signaled the rest of the squad that we were in position. This took place after the new LT had threatened us all with court marshals for not obeying his orders to proceed across the open field. The LT along with the gun team and his RTO started across the open ground. We had our weapons trained at the top of the clearing where we thought the ambush might spring from.

The gun team led out with the LT walking fourth man carrying his M-16 by the carrying handle like it was a brief case. They had covered about fifty yards when they came under fire from up the hill. We immediately returned fire while our exposed squad members hit the ground and sought positions to bring their M-60 into action. Four of us were able to place fully automatic fire on the enemy positions while our M-79 man placed well aimed HE rounds into the midst of them. The ambush was broken up in very short order, and no one on our side was hit. The guys caught in the open all returned fire, that is, except for the new LT. We advanced through the brush to the ambush site. While clearing the area, several blood trails were found, and some drag marks. They led off the side of the ridge where we were reluctant to follow. We spent about an hour searching the area for the rocket launch site. It consisted of a camp site where a half a dozen men might have camped. There was bamboo scaffolding that we figured was used to hold the rocket that was being launched. We were finding more and more trails off the sides of the ridge indicating that there were greater numbers of NVA in the area. We moved back down the ridge until we had come up to our extraction point.

The new LT did not speak about court marshals after that, but the damage had been done. None of us trusted him. Guys began to talk about ways to get rid of him. A pool of money was up to four hundred dollars for the guy who would wound him in a fire fight. When Mike and I were talking to the company commander, I told him about it. The new LT was gone the next day, transferred out.

We were back on FSB Arsenal, our home out of the bush. Word had come down that the base was going to be hit in the next few nights. The next day was spent reinforcing the bunker line and repairing the perimeter defenses. We would work in shifts alternating between working on the defenses and guarding the other guys who were doing the work.

ON LOAN TO A SISTER PLATOON

Sergeant Berry called Myler and me over to his bunker. We were both RTO's, and it turned out that one of the platoons was short a Delta One, and since we had an extra, one of us was going to have to volunteer to go with them. The general rule of survival in Nam was, "Never volunteer for anything".

Myler and I argued back and forth as to who was to go and I wound up stepping forward. Sergeant Berry dismissed Myler and said, "You idiot, if you would have held your ground for a few minutes, I'd have made Myler go. You are the senior RTO, but now you are going." "You will catch the next bird going to FSB Birmingham where you will report to LT Muellenbach. I shouldered my gear and made my way to the chopper pad thinking, "What the heck, it was just one mission."

When my bird dropped in to Birmingham, I reported in to LT Muellenbach. Standing before him, I realized he was a guy I had known from our platoon a few weeks earlier. He came in as a Shake and Bake E-5 and had been field commissioned to LT just days ago. He had gone from squad leader to platoon sergeant to LT platoon leader in a very short time.

Our company commander was Captain Arrington. He had been our CO for some months and seemed pretty squared away. On this mission we would have The Flag, which is the CO, along with the LT. I would serve as the LT's RTO. I was there to replace an RTO who was called home for a convalescent leave. Word was that his mother had died, and he was granted leave to go to the funeral.

Our mission would take us out to an area between the Asha Valley and FSB Ripcord, out near the border with Laos. I had been out to that general area before and knew that it was used regularly by the NVA and that anyone going out there better have their shit together.

To begin, I feel I need to give you some context. It has been forty-three years since this mission took place. Many of the details such as individuals' names, I have forgotten or just never knew. I was on loan to this platoon for one mission beginning on or about the end of July 1970. We were an understrength platoon. As I recall, twenty-two of us boarded the birds that would insert us on a hill out near the border.

We hit the ground without taking any fire. After checking out the LZ and establishing the order of march, we followed the point man off the hill in single file. I was near the center of the line behind the LT. We moved down a ridgeline crossing several good-sized trails, trails that were deeply worn and recently traveled. The more we went downhill; the more enemy sign we saw. From time to time we would hear the distant sound of a truck motor or the chopping sound from someone felling trees. That first night we found a good NDP, night defensive position, on the crest of a ridge within direct line of fire to one of our fire bases. We had taken a lot of precautions to conceal our movements and as of yet did not think the NVA knew of our location. The following morning, we moved out of our NDP at first light and spent the beginning of the day probing toward the area west and north of our insertion point. The terrain we were in was mostly triple canopy jungle. So, although there was plenty of concealment, the going was extremely slow, and the temptation to use the trails was strong. Trails made the traveling much faster and easier, but the tradeoff was a much greater chance of detection, booby- traps, ambushes and fire fights.

Over the next two days several guys came down with malaria and had to be evacuated. On the fourth day of the mission we humped to an LZ and received resupply. On the resupply bird was the RTO I was there to replace. He took over my radio, and I became assistant machine-gunner for one of the gun teams. As it turned out his mother hadn't died; it had been his grandmother, so his leave was denied, and he was sent back to the field. Since the platoon was shorthanded, I was slated to finish the mission with them. This was my first time at being an assistant gunner. I was trained on the M-60 and had fired it numerous times in training and on fire bases, but up to this point had not been part of a gun team in combat. My gunner was Jim Blondell, from Smith River, Oregon. He told me what he expected from me if we were called upon in a fire fight. It would not be long before my new skills would be put to the test.

Our gun was at the rear of the column as we made our way down into the ravine. I carried two hundred rounds of 7.62 linked ammo in cans and another hundred rounds wound around the top of my ruck sack. The platoon moved with as much stealth as possible down towards the bottom of the canyon. The terrain we moved through was double and triple canopy jungle. It had rained for a while last night, and it was the time of morning when the temperature begins to rise and with it the steam carrying the smells from the jungle floor. I caught a whiff of canned fish that let me know that our adversaries had their breakfast. At the bottom of the ravine we came onto a large trail. The point and the rest of the platoon were all on the trail by the time we stepped onto it. We hadn't moved more than fifty yards when the point man took a trail watcher under fire. The platoon took up defensive positions while the lead element checked out the trail watcher and secured the area along our direction of travel. The dead trail watcher was searched for intelligence information and the body left by the side of the trail. We moved deeper into the canyon.

The platoon reached a place where a side canyon came in from the left at a Y in the trail. It was decided that we would move on to the right side of the Y and set up a defensive position while the point team made a short reconnaissance up the left side. We were in the process of setting up when an ambush was blown on the point team. From my position on the left of the M-60, I linked up another hundred rounds as we prepared to take on targets to our front. Hundreds of rounds of NVA fire were cracking through the air. The point team was down, and we couldn't see them or the enemy. At the Y in the canyon the jungle was only about thirty feet high, but extremely thick. We laid down a base of fire in the general direction that the fire was coming from while trying to ascertain the status of the point team. During a lull in the firing, I raised up to throw a grenade. As I got up to throw, I could see a questioning look in the eyes of several of the guys nearest to me. I could hear the whack of bullets passing through the vegetation above me and to my left. I threw the grenade as high and far as I could. I saw it arch over the first of the trees. Its forward momentum halted maybe twenty feet from my position. As it tumbled lamely to the ground, the whole team hugged the earth to avoid its deadly fragments. It exploded harming neither us nor the NVA. The point team made it back to us by low crawling in a shallow swale that paralleled the trail they had gone up.

The ambush had been fired a few seconds early when only the point man had entered the kill zone. By going to ground, only the point man's rucksack could be seen by the NVA. As they concentrated their fire on his rucksack, he slipped out of it and was able to back out of the kill zone. Firing ceased from the ambush site, and the NVA melted back into the jungle.

Our presence in the area was well known by then, so the decision was made to get out of the AO before a larger force could be gathered together to come looking for us. We backtracked to an NDP site not far from where we had spent the previous night. That was the night of August the fourth, nineteen-seventy. On the way to our NDP site we were able to get resupplied and medivac several people.

My memory of that evening is of absolute exhaustion. The adrenalin rush that lasted for hours, the humping of equipment into and out of that canyon, and the expectation that we would be called upon to do it again tomorrow.

Our platoon had been winnowed down to just fourteen of us. We passed the night unmolested and were back on the move at dawn of the fifth. Our gun team was just behind the point with the point man, one slack man guarding the point, then our machine gunner, Jim, then me. Most of the guys in this unit called me Fred. The remainder of the unit was LT Muellenbach, Captain Arrington, their RTO's, then another gun team that doubled as rear security. We packed as much gun ammo as we could carry, as did every other man that wasn't carrying a radio.

Our mission for the day was to probe back down into the same area as the day before. We moved as silently as we could descending back into the canyon by a different route than we had gone yesterday.

It was hot out and past noon when we neared the bottom of the canyon. There was very little of the usual jungle sounds; instead, every once in a while, I would hear a distant sound like chopping or a muffled clink, like someone dropped a canteen cup way off. Our eyes and ears strained to penetrate the terrain around us. Those of us who recognized it could smell the body odor and cooking fires of our enemy. We spent several hours trying to search the area without using the trails. Whispered messages moved up and down the line as the LT passed words to the point and was answered back. The point man came to a small, step across stream, and the decision was made to go up it. Now I was walking fourth man behind the point, slack and machine gunner. Rounding a slight turn in the creek the point man's arm came up as a signal to stop. Peering past the gunner up toward the area in front of the point, I could see a pith helmet setting on the bank next to the stream. On top of it was a bar of soap still wet from use. It caught the light of the sun trickling through the canopy overhead. Time froze, and we could hear the sing song sound of Vietnamese being spoken in light conversation and laughter. It took us a few seconds to realize that the sound was coming from a hole in the bank about fifteen feet over our heads.

Jim and I set the gun up covering the entrance to the hole while the point and slack took up positions to our left. The point man signaled back to have the M-79 man come up. We figured to pop a grenade in on them and end the party. When our M-79 man made it up to our position, we pointed out to him the hole in the bank that the sounds were coming from. He took up a position just below the hole and expertly laid a round of (HE), high explosive, right on target.

The HE round must travel so far, turning so many revolutions to arm itself, we were too close. Four of us opened up with three M-16s and the M-60 as small arms began to fire down on us from concealed fighting trenches to the left and right of the hole. My first job was to keep a belt of ammo linked up, so the gunner had an uninterrupted supply. If the gun jammed or the gunner had to change barrels, it was my job to fill in with my M-16 while he could get the gun back online. The firing was so intense that we had to maintain a continuous rate of fire in order to keep their heads down. As I knelt next to Jim to link up another belt, sticks and leaves rained down all around from the bullets passing just over our heads.

Guys were passing up fresh ammo, and we had gone through at least one barrel when an NVA stood up in the fighting trench to our left front with an RPG. I had just laid down my weapon in order to link up another belt. I managed to link it and was reaching to bring my weapon to bear as I looked in to the eyes of the man with the rocket on his shoulder. I could see his hand tighten on the trigger as I fought to bring my weapon up. I saw the bloom as the rocket left its tube. Rounds were still leaving the M-60 as Jim and I went flying through the air.

I thought, this is what it is like to die. Coming to on the ground, I saw Jim crawling back to his machine gun. He got the thing back up and firing, and I got back at his side feeding the gun.

By this time nearly all of the vegetation had been stripped away between us and the NVA positions. We had put over a thousand rounds through the gun. The surviving enemy was still able to bring inaccurate fire to bear by holding their weapons up out of their fighting positions and firing in our general direction. Somewhere near twelve hundred rounds, a round cooked off in the feed tray rendering the gun inoperable. Jim said, "Run!" and we all picked up and made it back around the bend in the creek without getting killed. As soon as we were far enough back, gunships made several runs at the hidden bunker with rockets and mini guns. After that the resistance from that position ceased.

Jim had taken shrapnel from the RPG while I came through it with just powder burns. A resupply helicopter brought us out a new M-60 and more ammo. Jim rode in to the med station with them. I moved into the machine gunner's spot and was joined by Earl as my assistant gunner. Earl had just three days left in country. He had lost his rucksack when we were ambushed several days before. Our gun was behind the point when we went back up to the bunker location to check it out.

The bunker location had been decimated by the air strike. Pieces of bodies and weapons was all I saw. My bell had been rung pretty hard by the RPG earlier. My vision was ok, but my hearing was just coming back online. By now it was getting towards evening. We had perhaps a half hour before sun set. There was a loach flying over the crest of the hill above us. Someone from there informed the LT that NVA were moving down the hill away from us and that we should move in that direction. We formed up and humped to the top of the hill. At the crest we found a network of trails with one leading off towards the valley in the direction that the fleeing NVA had taken.

After searching the top of the hill, the Lt and Captain Arrington formed us up to follow the trail following the NVA. My gun was with the point team, so I would be walking third man in the order of march. I spoke to the Lt, saying we should not probe down into the valley this late in the day. He replied that we were ordered down into the valley and that I should take my gun to the rear. My first reaction was to protest. Then I thought twice about it and concluded that he might be more assured by having his more experienced gunner at the front. After all, I had only been a gunner for about an hour at that time. I took my gun to the rear with Earl as my assistant gunner and gave the other gunner the word that he was to take his team to the front.

There were thirteen of us on that trail as we stepped off into the valley. Our line stretched out as we established our interval to move down the trail. We had only been moving for a few minutes when a break was called. Earl had to take a dump, so I positioned myself to where I could see behind us back up the trail and still see the next man in the column. A message passed from the front, "Send up a LAW" (66mm anti-tank weapon)." I sent back down, "There is no LAW." As I looked down the trail, I could see that the point had moved onto a larger trail that bisected the one we were on. I could see wheel tracks where an anti-aircraft gun had been moved through the area. I thought, "What the hell are they doing on a major trail like that?" Earl was still taking care of business when I heard the front gun open up. Six rounds cleared the front gun when a series of explosions tore across the trail below me. Small arms fire began to crack from off to the right as smoke and dust and leaves boiled from under the canopy. From below I heard, "Get the gun up here! Get that other fucking gun up here!"

I called to Earl and began to move forward. I managed to get my gun to the bottom of the hill and set up in a circle of teak wood trees that offered a decent defensive position. Several of the walking wounded filled in the gaps between the trees and were returning fire in the direction to our front. At this point, Earl reached my position and said, "Fred, I can't go up there, I got two days left in country." I took his M-16 to go forward while he continued to organize our position and provide covering fire.

On my first trip up to the front, crawling and moving from cover to cover, I came by several more walking wounded and sent them in the direction of Earl's position. Our sole remaining RTO was covered with gore and in shock. I reached over and keyed his mike, and the TOC came up on the set. I handed him the mic and said, "Get us gunships; get us medevac; get us extraction, and get back to the gunner." The next thing I came to was Captain Arrington lying against the base of a huge teakwood tree. He looked like he had been blown there by the force of a mine that had gone off only a few feet from him. What was left of the lieutenant lay only several feet away, Captain Arrington said, "Check Lt Muellenbach's pulse." So, I placed my fingers to his neck and said, "He's dead, sir. He's dead." Both of his legs were gone along with one of his arms. The other one came off as one of the walking wounded, and I rolled him into his poncho. The three of them pulled the poncho back towards our defensive position.

The front gunner, who had taken my place perhaps an hour before, lay next to the trail where he had fallen. I can't remember how, but we managed to get him in to the circle of teakwood trees. By this time there were gunships circling the area and a medivac was taking guys up on a jungle penetrator. I needed to make one more trip to the front to retrieve an M-16 that I had seen on a previous trip. I was still partly deaf from earlier in the day, and the small arms fire that crackled through the trees sounded like it was traveling through jello. I crawled the last few yards to the front to where I had seen the M-16. As I peeked around the base of huge teakwood, I could see that the M-16 had been blown in half. Only the butt end of the stock was in view. From that position I could see into a bunker complex. I counted nine bunkers, and people moving around like ants on an ant hill. I got my head back around that tree and headed for our position. I arrived back there in time to take my turn at giving mouth to mouth to the LT's RTO.

When the mines went off, he had been hit from the front. Pieces of the smoke grenades that he carried on his gear were blown into his body as far as his lungs. Each time we would blow air into him it would ignite the particles of smoke grenade (made of white phosphorous), so that he exhaled purple smoke. He was on fire inside, and the smell was overwhelming, causing us to have to trade off after every couple of breaths. He spoke incoherently about his mom as various ones worked over him. He was alive as they lifted him out, tied to the jungle penetrator.

By now it was getting dark. We used a strobe light to signal the bird where to drop the penetrator. I kept moving from Earl, who was still firing from time to time, to the extraction point. Everyone had gotten out except Earl and I… and a body bag with about thirty pounds of the LT in it. I called Earl to the extraction point and realized that the strobe light had been taken up with the last man. Earl and I tried to signal the bird with a flashlight, but it wasn't bright enough to be seen through the canopy. In an effort to find us the pilot turned on his search light. We could see him above us, but so could the NVA as they opened up on him with an antiaircraft gun. Tracers the size of pumpkins were streaming up at them from the NVA position. They had no choice but to pull out.

Earl and I crouched in the extraction point with the M-60 machinegun, an M-16, a PRC-25 radio, my rucksack and the body bag. We made a quick decision to go back up the trail we had come down being as that was the only terrain we were familiar with, and it would get us out of the area fast. Dragging the body bag between us we headed up the hill. As we exited, we could hear movement below us. We ran as fast as our burdens would allow to the top of the ridge line. At the crown of the hill was a field of thick brush extending all around for several hundred yards. We had passed it earlier in the day. We burrowed into the thick mass pulling our gear and the bag of the LT with us. We did our best in the dark to cover the hole where we entered the brush pile. Earl and I continued to squirm through the brush until we reached the apex of the ridgeline that we were on. We found a slight depression and set up there pointing the gun back in the direction we had come. We laid quiet for what seemed like a long time, trying to get our breathing under control.

I had just turned my attention to the radio when we heard movement around our brush pile. Earl and I tried to remain calm while grenades and incendiaries were thrown into the pile. We had burrowed in far enough as to be beyond the reach of hand grenades. Our fear was that the pile would burn. Fortunately for us, it was too wet.

I figured there wasn't one NVA in a thousand that wanted to start crawling through that brush on his belly in the dark of night on the off chance that he could engage me and Earl in a little one on one. The noise around us calmed down as the search moved away up the ridgeline.

At this time in my tour I had been carrying the radio for about seven months. I had become competent in its use and familiar with its limitations. Most RTO's in the field had a Wiz-wheel. It was a thin plastic device with a face a little like a rotary phone dial. With it I could code and decode secure messages.

As soon as I began to raise the TOC, I could hear strange squelch coming up on the frequency. Every radio has a voice that is a little different. When you break squelch by keying your mike, you hear that voice. To a lesser degree, you also hear it when you change frequency or when another radio comes up on the frequency you are on.

As I tried to reach the TOC to call in our location and let them know we were alive, I could hear through the radio the enemy monitoring our freak. I would send quick coded messages to try and beat the enemy RTO and keep him from being able to triangulate with his RTO's to figure out our position. It took until about midnight before I was sure the TOC had our position and were appraised of our situation.

Staring into the black wall of brush around us, Earl and I hunkered down listening to the sounds of small animals and night birds. Hoping that the enemy was not nearby listening for us to give away our position, we were able to talk in whispers in between listening to the enemy making noises from far off as the search continued for us. Our biggest fear was that they would have tracker dogs. We didn't know if the NVA even had service dogs, but if they did this would sure be an opportunity to put them to work.

Earl kept saying," Two days and a wake up," or "What am I doing here?" If there was any kind of justice in this world he should have been setting at the EM-club with a beer getting ready to Sky. A grunt's worst fear is to make it almost all the way through his tour and then to be killed or wounded on the day or two before he goes home. Seconds passed like hours as we sat back to back peering into the dark and catching the smell of war and death that emanated from the body bag a few feet away.

At about two AM I began to receive a transmission from the TOC. Once again, I had to play cat and mouse with the enemy RTO's but was able after much running up and down the dials to put together their message. A LURP (long range recon patrol) was on the same ridgeline as us about a thousand meters farther up. They were willing to try and link up with us by moving down the ridgeline to our position. They brought their radio onto our push, and we broke and returned two squelch breaks every fifteen minutes to signal, "Situation normal." Just before dawn Earl and I were straining our ears in the direction the LURPs should be coming from. At this point we had been on high alert for twenty-four hours. We could hear shuffling and rustling in the brush as we aimed our weapon in the direction of the noise, noise that was so similar to what we had been hearing all night. Sounds from the NVA still found their way to us from other directions. I was straining so hard to hear, over the sound of my breathing and the heart beating in my chest. Was the sound right in front of me coming from small animals, the enemy, or my buddies coming to link up with us? We were coming up on time for a SITREP (situation report). I keyed my mike twice, and then listening with all my might, I could hear on the night air the sound of the LURP radio breaking squelch. I spoke softly towards the noise, "Lurps." Seconds passed, and I heard a reply; "Grunts." At that moment a belief that we might survive sprung back into the realm of possibility. Little did I realize, it was a four-man LURP- team. It was still a long wait until dawn even with four more guys and another radio.

I had been plotting artillery targets all around us on the ridge in preparation for whatever might happen in the morning. Peeking out of our brush pile after dawn we found no enemy in the immediate area. We would be extracted by helicopter after prepping it with an artillery strike.

The senior NCO of the LURP team was a black E-7 I had seen a few times back at Evens or coming on or off of fire bases. He looked to be in his mid to late thirties, and I couldn't help but think, "What is this old guy doing out here?" We spoke for a while, and he said I looked like a kid.

The LURPs seemed to have better intel than us and were informed that the whole battalion was taken out of the field for a Stand Down. We were a day late to the party. As soon as we hit the ground, I was to be present at a battalion formation, and Earl would be processing out of Vietnam.

We called in an artillery strike on the area around the LZ where our extraction would be that lifted just before our birds came in. A company was coming in to work over the AO. A Captain asked me, "See any gooks around here?" I told him, "Sir, when you step off of this ridge, if you go down into that valley, there are Boo-Koo NVA. Expect a fight."

Earl and I boarded the third bird as it discharged its load. Earl held his breath, as did I, and the bird took on lift as it began to gather forward motion. The bottoms of my feet tingled in expectation as the ground dropped away. Our eyes searched the jungle below for a sign of anything that might prevent our safe departure. When we were high above the jungle and cutting through clean air toward the rear, Earl leaned over to yell in my ear, "One Day and a Wake up!"

When we reached camp Evans, Earl and I caught a ride to our company area. He began processing out, while I dropped my gear and was told to go to be part of a battalion formation. Walking onto the parade field, I saw that the companies and platoons were all formed up in neat ranks and rows forming the various units within the battalion. I found the place where the platoon I had been with should be and realized I was the only one there to represent the platoon. Earl was processing out, and all the rest were in the aid stations or hospital or dead. I stood there to the right of center, front row as the sun beat down on the sand that covered the parade grounds. Our commander and various ones spoke from a raised platform to our front. They droned on about what a successful operation it had been and how well we had performed in the field. I was teetering on the edge of passing out from exhaustion. The speaker informed us that we would all have a couple of days at Eagle Beach as part of our week of stand down. The rest of the week would be given over to classes on the latest mines and booby traps that the enemy had been developing to use on us, getting our gear in shape, zeroing our weapons and in general honing the skills of the infantry man.

The speaker put us at ease and came down from the podium. He began to walk over to me and as he approached, I realized he was the voice in the helicopter that ordered us down into the valley the day before. He began to speak to me in person. My anger rose in my throat as I thought of the men who had perished to follow his request. Just then, Jim Blondell, the other gunner who was wounded the day before walked up. The colonel turned his attention to him just as I was about to blow my top. I wanted to scream at him while ripping his guts out. The tension of the past days, my complete exhaustion and the sun beating down on the parade field coupled with the fact that I hadn't showered or bathed in several weeks all seemed to catch up with me at once.

"Diaper Dan! Diaper Dan!" penetrated my brain from two platoons over. "You made it! Man, you made it!" The guys from my regular platoon saw me standing there and came running over to welcome me back. All they knew was that the platoon I was with had suffered many casualties. They had assumed by the numbers that I had been one of them. We went from there to our company area where there was cold beer and familiar faces. I never saw or heard from Earl again.   He Skied!

Over the next several days we sat through classes on first aid and squad tactics, until it was our turn to go to Eagle Beach. We packed into the back of duce-and-halfs for the ride through Hue to the South China Sea. From there we boarded landing craft that ferried us out to Tan My Island where the Screaming Eagles had their stand down area. For two full days we drank and smoked pot, laid on the beach, and caught the USO show that played twice a day.

I managed to lay on the beach for most of those two days, licking my wounds over having lost my girlfriend. There wasn't so much of a dear-john letter as a series of hints about going to concerts with friends, staying out all night and dropped hints about the boys back home. On the second morning I came to in a deck chair on the beach. A dog woke me up digging in the sand near my chair. He came up with a plastic bag, and a guy called him over and took the bag. "What is this?" I asked. The guy came over and plopped down in the sand next to me. "Oh, you've just met, Big Head. One of the cadres here at the stand down area got him to sniff for pot some time ago. Every night guys sit out on this beach getting stoned, and whenever an officer or NCO come walking by, they shove their stash down in the sand to avoid getting busted. A lot of them can't find their goods or pass out and forget about it.

You may ask how did Big Head get trained to find pot? The story I heard was that one of the cadres trained him a couple of years ago, and he has been doing it ever since. All of us here are grunts who have served our time in the field and are in the last month or so of our tour. As our tours come to an end, we pass Big Head's story onto the next head and his skills carry on. Big Head gets at least one hamburger a day from the canteen and whatever scraps he can get. Big Head is a happy dog, and as far as I know, no officers or anyone above the rank of buck sergeant, are aware of his unique skills. We never have to buy pot, because Big Head keeps us supplied."

Big Head was built really thick, unlike many of the Vietnamese dogs. He had a head that looked too big for his body. He didn't care much to be petted or scratched except while accepting a snack. He seemed to know that we were transients here and long relationships were not part of the deal. He served in his way as we did in ours. My new friend handed me the bag Big Head had dug up next to my chair. "Enjoy the last day of your time at the beach," he said as he and Big Head walked away down the beach.

The next morning, we were at the landing for our ride back to the mainland, then boarded the cattle trucks for the ride back to base. Riding in the open truck through Hue City was an experience in itself. Modes of transport of all descriptions crowded the streets and intersections. Old French Citrons, bicycles, buffalo carts, motor scooters, jeeps, foot traffic, three wheeled trucks stacked high with villagers headed to town with pigs, chickens and produce, mixed with tanks, APC's, gun trucks and convoys. In the mix were cowboys on motorcycles. As I explained earlier, "Cowboy" was a miss interpretation of the Vietnamese word, cowoy, which means thief. These Cowboys would ride two to a motorbike weaving in and out of the open vehicles. They would snatch wristwatches off the wrists of unsuspecting GI's. It was amazing how adept they were at their trade. We had all been warned of the possibility of a grenade being thrown into our truck, so although we tried to relax and enjoy the show, we remained locked and loaded.

When our trucks pulled into base, we stowed our gear and went for hot chow. Afterward there was to be a formation in the company area and a ceremony to honor those we had lost during the past several missions. It was over a hundred degrees as we stood in formation to honor our dead. Next to where the speaker stood was a low table. On it were three pairs of spit shined boots and three helmets to represent the three lives that were no more on this earth. As the speaker droned on, I couldn't help but think. They were grunts. They hadn't worn a spit shined boot or a shined helmet since arriving in Vietnam. It was our privilege to honor them one last time in this formal way.

We were dismissed to our company area to check our gear and get ready for our next mission. Back at the company area the beer came out as we sat around smoking and joking the afternoon away. A big topic was the Vietnamization of the war. It had come down from on high that we were to go to the field with the South Vietnamese Army, in order to prepare them to take over the roles we were now filling. We all wanted to hand our jobs over to them, but none of us was confident they could pull it off. We had been on missions with our counterparts where when we began to get close to the enemy they just disappeared, just walked back to their village to avoid the fight. Apparently, they knew what we were reluctant to learn - that the NVA had no quit in them. They would keep sending troops down the Ho Chi Min trail for as long as it took, even if they never won a battle. This was while our leaders at the highest levels argued over the shape of the negotiation table and wouldn't bomb targets in the north or cross borders into Cambodia or Laos.

Many of the South Vietnamese were wonderful, dedicated soldiers that I had the pleasure of serving alongside. By August of 1970 the majority of boots on the ground could see the way things were going. It looked like a free democratic South Vietnam was not going to emerge from this mass of corruption that made up the government of the South or the American leadership they were partnered with.

How can I explain to this generation what it was like to prepare for the next mission? To fill 21 magazines with 5.56, to pack your claymores and grenades, to be at your best physically, mentally and emotionally. To go face an enemy that has been at war for longer than you've been alive. One who will place sharpened bamboo dipped in feces in a pit in order to give you a bad day.

Our kill ratio was ten to one. Various celebrities of the time supported us while others called us baby killers and publicly embraced our enemy. Many prominent news people came out against the war… and by proxy us. We were hated on the college campus and reviled by academia. Racial tension was exacerbated by such terms as," I don't want to fight the white man's war." The Black Panthers sent their message to be spread by the parasites that sought to infest the disenfranchised. The woman's right's movement and sexual revolution did their part to call into question the value of manhood and family structure.

Our few days in the rear reminded us of the complex world we lived in but did little to soften the reality of going back to the field, to the simple but terrifying mission of surviving to come home.

On the day before we were to go back to the bush, I was called to go before the Battalion XO (executive officer). As I waited outside his office, I wondered what brand of trouble I had gotten myself into this time. Standing before him, I was struck dumb for several seconds. Here was Captain Arrington sitting behind his desk, looking uninjured. A week ago, I had helped him back to the lift zone to be taken out on the jungle penetrator. Apparently, the blood and gore that he was covered with were not his, but that of Lieutenant Muellenbach. I could hear his voice speaking and fought to think clearly and listen to what he was saying. He was offering me a chance to get out of the bush and to take a post as an RTO with a Green Beret team working out of a small base with 175 South Vietnamese and 6 Americans. No more humping the bush with a rucksack, I'd be sleeping on a cot. I accepted the change of duty and was released back to my company. Transportation would be provided for me after morning chow the next day.

I was able to spend one more evening with my old platoon. Everyone was happy with beer, sodas and mail from home. The usual card games broke out, and I was just getting into one when Sergeant Berry questioned my sanity as to throwing in with the Green Berets. He said he knew of the base and although it was nearby, it had been hit pretty regularly and might not be as secure as I was led to believe. At around eleven, Mike and I and a few of the heads stepped outside and went into an empty hooch to smoke a bomber and shoot the breeze. Everyone had plenty of advice for me as to my new assignment. I hit the rack not long after that and laid awake for a few minutes wondering what I had fallen into this time.

My ride to my new assignment wouldn't be along for several hours, so I boarded a truck out to the chopper pad with my platoon to watch them load up and head back to the field. As it turned out, that would be the last time I would see many of them. Some of them had finished their tours and gone stateside by the time I would rejoin the platoon   Most just skied. I'd never know what happened to them.

A jeep pulled up outside the company headquarters. I got in beside the driver, known as Wild Bill, and we blasted down the road leaving Phu Bia towards Birmingham. As it turned out, I would ride with Wild Bill many times and come to appreciate how he got his name. Wild Bill didn't drive slowly, no time for nobody. His theory on staying alive was that a moving target was hard to hit, and the faster the target moved the better. He managed to get the maximum performance out of that little, pressed metal jeep at all times. He dumped me at the gate opening into the old French fortification that was my new assignment and raised a cloud of dust back toward Phu Bia. With my M-16 and a bandolier of ammo, I made my way across a small parade field to a concrete building with the letters HQ painted next to the opening where there had at one time been a door. When I darkened the opening, I was waved inside by one of the three guys setting inside. I stood there confused wondering who I was supposed to report to. Two of the guys looked to be in their late thirties, and none of them wore any rank. I stated that I was to report to LT Bingham as his RTO. The youngest of the three, a Green Beret sergeant by the name of Macon, stepped up to welcome and brief me. Together we walked around the perimeter of the little base. It had been built in the fifties by the French to maintain a presence along the Song Tra Bong, a river that flowed from out near the Lao border through Phu Bia to the South China Sea. It was just on the upriver side of a small village that adjoined the river at Pohl Bridge. Macon explained to me that the base was a South Vietnamese installation, with a population that hovered a little under two hundred, mostly new recruits that would leave from here to become replacements in local army units. It was apparent that the base had been hit recently by the number of bullet holes and mortar and RPG scars that pock - marked the area. Our building was missing about a quarter of its roof due to mortar fire. The rocket holes had been patched with brick and plaster but had not been painted yet. The previous RTO (Paul) that I was replacing had been wounded in the attack the week before.

Macon took me over to the commo bunker and introduced me around to my Vietnamese counterparts. There would be six South Vietnamese Army, RTO's, an interpreter, and myself in the bunker during the twelve hours a day that I was on duty. It was a type of bunker construction that was present on most of the firebases made with sand bags, ammo boxes and runway matting. Bristling with radio antennas, it sat just inside the front gate. There was one door into the bunker with no firing ports or other means of egress. A generator in an adjacent building supplied power for lights and the land lines that connected phones around the base.

Walking back to our quarters, Macon explained to me that I could leave or enter the base at any time that I wasn't on duty and that the village just outside the gate had a little store, and a restaurant run by a woman named Thue who was fair to deal with and liked GI's. He recommended keeping my forays outside the base to daylight hours at least till I became familiar with my new surroundings. He showed me where to stash my gear and gave me a cot in the same room that he bunked in. Some of the roof tiles were missing, so we kept our cots along the opposite wall. Just to the left outside our quarters was a 30-foot guard tower, where at least one American kept watch at all times. Beside my radio watches I'd have other duties added to my things to do over time.

At six that evening my first radio watch began. I was told by Macon that I would meet LT Bingham in the morning.

As I entered the commo bunker it took a few seconds for my eyes to adjust to the light. I was introduced to the other RTOs by my interpreter,Then, and sat down in front of a bank of radios to begin monitoring the traffic. We had six Green Beret teams that we worked with out of that bunker. Each team consisted of two Americans, and anywhere from half a dozen to forty indigenous tribal people, Mung or Motan Yards. They were west of us out along the border conducting various operations that kept them in the field for extended periods of time. My function was to receive their requests for resupply, medivac or transport and relay those requests to make sure they had what they needed.

I had been at my new task for several hours when the door to the bunker sprung open and in walks a Vietnamese woman in her early twenties looking good. She walked straight over to me and asked in broken English, "Where Paul?" The Vietnamese RTOs and I were handling a lot of radio traffic, so there was a buzz of incoming and outgoing traffic in at least two languages. I was likely the only nonsmoker in the bunch, so she came close to me through a veil of smoke, close enough so that I could smell her perfume. She placed her hand upon my shoulder and asked again, "Where Paul?" I noticed in the background some growing discussion, and my interpreter left the room. I told the woman that I was Paul's replacement and that he had been wounded and sent home. Tears ran down her face as she said, "I love him so much. He number one GI." Then she came a little closer and said, "You want be my babe san?" All of this was going on while I listened and responded to radio traffic. My mind was racing with all that I'd been through in the past several weeks when the door burst open and in from the dark comes my interpreter, Then, and the biggest Vietnamese I had ever seen. This guy was about six feet tall and built like a fullback. He grabbed the girl and proceeded to knock the shit out of her as he drug her outside. I asked Then, "What is going on?" He says, "That girl is a whore and a spy and will be interrogated." The rest of that night my mind raced between doing my job on the radio, and the images of the girl being hauled off.

My watch came to an end at six in the morning. As I made my way to my bunk, I saw the woman naked in a barbwire cage on the ground. It was obvious that she had been violated far beyond what could be considered interrogation. I went to one of the old guys, who I assumed was the ranking member of the Americans there. I told him about the girl and what had taken place the previous night at the commo bunker. His answer was that we were guests there. This was their base. She was their prisoner. We had no say in it. After three days she was no longer in the cage. I heard nothing more on the subject. Sometimes, I can still smell her perfume, as she placed her hand on my shoulder in that smoke-filled bunker and said, "You want be my babe san?"

On the morning of my second day at the fort, I met LT Bingham. He was laying on his cot when a call came up on the radio from HQ. I was mobile with a PRC-25, but I was not in the commo-bunker. The call would come out every morning at the same time. It was like a conference call sending general information to everyone on the call list. It required that each person answer up to their call sign to acknowledge reception. I held the hand set up to Bingham's ear so that he could receive the call. After returning his call sign, he rolled over and disregarded the rest of the call. His eyes didn't seem to focus properly, and unless he made a special effort, his speech wasn't intelligible. Later that day I was able to ask Macon, "What, was going on?" He said that Bingham had been out on the border with the Yards for too long. He had gone native. It would take him some time to come back to our reality. Part of my job as his RTO would be to cover for him until he came around. If he was sent back to the rear right now, he would most likely be put in a mental ward and that would be the end of his career. It wasn't without precedent. Other team members over the years had come back from the bush in the same condition. This was a way of giving him a chance to come out of it. Most did in time.

Every few days, one of the teams would wander into the fort. They would look like a band of Indians from an old western. There would be Mama Sans with purple to black stained teeth from chewing betel nut, along with the men who carried a variety of weapons and dressed in traditional clothing that looked like they made it themselves. They would be around for a few hours to get supplies, before melting back into the jungle. Yards and other native people were held in contempt by the Vietnamese people in general. They were considered savages and treated poorly. I remember they seemed much more ready to smile than the Vietnamese. They were forest people and jungle people. That was their strength.

After being at my new assignment for a few days, the new routine was becoming comfortable. When I could, I would walk into the village to get a break. It felt good to hear children as I walked past the school. Although it too was pockmarked with bullet holes and patches from rocket fire, it was surrounded by an intricately woven fence made of barbed wire. On this day I met Theu for the first time. I was in front of her shop checking out the merchandise set out on tables under an awning. She stood in the dark of her shop observing me, her only customer. After a few moments she stepped out into the light to introduce herself. Over the forthcoming weeks I would come to realize what a fine friend she was. She asked if I would like a bowl of soup and led me back through the shop to some tables with window openings that caught a bit of breeze off the river. She brought my soup and took a seat near enough to talk. I would come to know that Theu was from Laos and besides her native tongue, spoke French, Vietnamese and English. She was fifty-two years old, and her parents had moved here from Laos when she was a girl. The shop, restaurant and home, where she now lived, had been her parents. She came into possession of it when her parents and siblings all passed away. She and her husband and two sons had been here all together during Tet of 68. All three of her men were home on leave from the SVA. Their house was surrounded in the night by many NVA. She was beaten and raped in front of her husband and sons before they were tortured, mutilated and beheaded in front of her. Somehow in spite of all that, she was able to remain calm, warm and welcoming to those who came to her door. As we talked, children below school age came in several times. They were given something to eat and their questions answered quietly. They looked upon me with interest and curiosity then melted into the surrounding rooms. Local SVA soldiers from the fort would wander in from time to time for a bowl of soup or a beer. Theu would serve them all then return to her seat and pick up the conversation where we left off. She came to represent to me the very best of what people can be.

Walking out of the shade at Theu's, I squinted to identify the SVA commander of the fort, setting at a table in the shade at a house across the street. He was a mean looking man with a red face and squinting eyes. I had observed him several times, addressing his troops at the fort. He looked back at me with contempt. I couldn't help but mistrust him given what had taken place the night of my arrival. What did I know? I'd just been at this new assignment for three days.

Everywhere I went I carried my M-16. Despite the relaxed attitude of the little base my bush mentality would not let me go without it. Even when I took a shower, I would place it where I could see it all the time. Off the base I would have at least eight magazines and a couple of frags in my pockets. There is nothing like a baseball size frag in your pocket to say, "Don't mess with me."

There was a sniper tower about a mile up the road from the base on our side of the river. Part of our job was to take them supplies and mail every three days. On those days, Wild Bill would show up in the afternoon and drive me, the mail and supplies to the tower. The tower sat back from the river about a hundred yards. It was built over the top of a bunker that housed a squad of SVA, who provided security for the snipers in the tower. I climbed up the ladder to the top and opened the hatch through the floor. Setting behind his M-14 sniper rifle was my friend Clyde. Seated next to him was his spotter Gene. I climbed up through the hole in the floor with Wild Bill right behind me. After closing the trap door to the ladder and delivering their mail and C-rations, I sat down on the floor to hear what Clyde had been up to since our last meeting on Birmingham.

Clyde sat to the left side of the tower facing out, with his right hand near the trigger of his M-14. As he spoke to me, he was constantly scanning the opposite side of the river and a trail that ran parallel to its bank. We talked about home and how our perspective on things changed as our tours went on. Clyde had recently been out along the border where a couple of infantry guys went missing. It was presumed that they had been captured. We speculated as to what might be happening to them. Our hope was that they would escape and find their way back to a friendly firebase. Clyde said that if they were captured, there wasn't much chance they would ever be heard from again. Crap, man, they were infantry E-3's, cannon fodder, no strategic value. Why would the NVA bother to march them all the way back up the Ho Chi Min trail? No, if you are a lowly infantry man you are much better off getting shot trying to escape than whatever fate awaits you at the hands of the NVA. I don't think there were too many infantry types occupying those prisons up north.

At that moment Clyde said, "I've got movement." Bam. One shot went down range. Clyde picked up the thread of conversation where we left off about being captured as an infantry man versus a pilot or a member of an air crew.

Light was fading fast, and we had to get back to base before dark. Wild Bill had to get back to the motor pool. We said our goodbyes to Clyde and Gene and burned down the road back to the fort.

Macon had the first watch that night, and since I wasn't sleepy, I climbed up to join him in the guard tower. From there we watched over the compound from above. Every couple of hours whoever was on watch would circle the fort to check on the various guard positions. Most of the time this involved waking up one or more SVA and admonishing them to stay alert.

I asked Macon about his take on what Clyde had said about the missing infantry men. Macon was on his third tour, his second with the Green Beret. He informed me that one of the more common practices among the NVA with prisoners of little value was to march them into the nearest village. There they would incite the locals against them and persuade them to beat the prisoners to death with sticks and stones. Once you've participated in caving in the skull of a tied, helpless prisoner, there is not much chance you won't spend the rest of your life trying to justify the act. By this method of handling the prisoners, manpower and money was saved, and loyalty to the leaders up north was further cemented in the minds and hearts of the people. According to Macon, very few infantry men ever lived long enough after being captured to see the inside of an NVA prison.

The next morning, I was in the communications bunker at six handling traffic from the teams and messages coming into the fort. I was told by my interpreter that an SVA patrol sent out along the opposite bank of the river that morning was coming back in with one kill. They had found the NVA dead on the trail opposite the sniper tower where I had been the night before when Clyde took his shot. It was at six hundred yards through the head in failing light. My appreciation for Clyde took a giant leap forward. This guy was a draftee, and had never fired a weapon before entering the army. When offered a commission to LT for one more year of service, he turned it down to become a grunt. His years at BYU studying psychology had given him an ability to speak about the war in a unique way. He could get to the essence of things without getting hung up in all of the political slant, either from the hippy left or the far right. Clyde was the embodiment to me of the citizen soldier. He made me hungry to be better and to develop my skills. He helped me to take pride in being a citizen soldier and to be one of the many who would do their best for one another.

One of Bingham's jobs was to fly Victor Romeo for the teams in the field. VR or variable reconnaissance was the job of flying over a team while maintaining radio communications with them. The team would want to know what was before them if at all possible. Since the LT was down, I filled in for him on most of the VR flights at that time. VR flights were considered non-combat, and out of our aviation unit were flown mostly by pilots just arrived in country from flight school. My understanding was that a new pilot had to log so many hours in country before he was eligible to fly combat missions. So, several days a week a LOH (light observation helicopter) and a pilot would pick me up, and we would log a couple of hours of flight time.

Most of these pilots were Warrant Officers and had a bullet proof attitude. We would be briefed as to the team we were to serve and their general location, then mount up and head that way. Most of the time we also carried mail and resupply. These LOH's (light observation helicopter) were unarmed, so I sat in the seat next to the pilot with my M-16, a gas mask bag full of magazines, and another bag full of hand grenades. Don was the first VR pilot I flew with, twenty-one years old from Santa Monica, California. He liked to fly nap of the earth. Our teams were to the west, so we would take off from the fort and fly up the river just a few feet off the water as fast as he could make it go. As the river got up into the mountains, the trees closed in on either side. Our pace didn't slow as we banked back and forth around the bends in the river. We followed a branch of the river to the north until we had to pop up out of the narrowing canyon. Now we were a much better target to anyone on the ground. We reached the area of the team, and they came up on the net. We were able to descend into a hole in the jungle and kick out their resupply. While I unloaded their stuff, I got a look at a few of the people pulling security around our LZ. I counted five of them not counting the one team member that stepped up to take the mail and ask that we recon to the west for a couple of clicks on our way out. I gave him an affirmative, and we popped back out of the hole we'd dropped into. We radioed back to the team that we had seen trails to the west and signs of recent use, but had spotted no actual enemy

Riding in the LOH was like riding a roller coaster. I could never get enough of it. Up until this point in my tour I had ridden in Huey's and CH-47's (Chinooks) and never in the front seat. This was a whole new level of flying. Being in the bubble I could see all around, above and below me, as the terrain tore past on all sides. By moving the stick a bit, Don could make the little bird fly sideways or backwards or almost upside down all while maintaining forward momentum. He wasn't afraid to fly that little bird into canyons and under trees. I'll always be thankful to the American Military for placing young men in those wonderful machines. To be fair, I saw it everywhere I went in Vietnam. Be they tankers, truck drivers, artillery men or riverine patrol guys. Young American men love their machines, and nearly every man will do all that they can to get the most out of them, to the point of recklessness. I never met a jeep driver worth his salt that didn't have a way to override the governor, so he could get a little more speed out of his unit.

Don came out to the fort and flew VR's several times after that before earning enough hours to fly combat missions. A string of other pilots followed each one as excited and dedicated to his craft as the one before. One of them picked me up one day and said, "Let's fly this route on out to the team." He had been shot at out in that area the day before and wanted to fly by it again. As we came up on the site from the previous day, I was ready with my M-16. I could hear the crack of AK fire between the sounds of my weapon over the noise of the LOH. I burned through 18 rounds having never seen a target, and we got the hell out of there. As we pulled out of the little canyon the pilot said, "I told you," as we laughed and enjoyed the adrenalin rush.

I was only one member of the team that took turns making the VR flights for LT Bingham. The others had been in the army a lot longer than me and had at least two tours in Nam. I don't think any of them got the enjoyment out of it that I did. My days at the fort became routine, with long radio watches and taking calls for Bingham. He didn't seem to be making much progress at coming out of his funk. As time went on, it became harder and harder to do the long radio watches in the commo bunker. Through my interpreter I was getting more and more out of the traffic that came over the SVA radios. I couldn't understand a lot more of the language, but each day, as I observed them, my confidence level as far as them succeeding against the NVA grew more tenuous. Also, the smell generated by eight of us in the bunker at times was so bad I thought I would gag if I had to deal with another minute of it. I would take a radio outside and pull my duty there as much as possible. Whenever I got a few hours off, I'd go into the village to Theu's place, have a cold drink and let her soothing voice quiet the demons that flew in and out of my head.

Theu was a Catholic. Somehow after all she had been through, she had been able to hang on to her faith and continue to pass on her love for Jesus.

After twenty-eight days at the fort we got hit. I was awake at midnight and carried my M-16 outside to take a leak. Macon spoke to me from up in the guard tower. "Hey Fred, come on up for a smoke." I climbed up the ladder and sat and smoked with Macon as we listened to the radio traffic and looked out over the perimeter. He said he had made the rounds twice and had caught the SVA guards at the far end of the base sleeping both times. At about 1 AM rounds started to crack at the far end of the perimeter. Grenades and small arms backed with mortar fire were hitting inside the wire at the far end of the base. I got on the radio and got up the TOC to let them know what was happening. On the ground below us, the other four members of our team and the interpreter were headed for the French Maid, a concrete bunker with a heavy steel door built when the French occupied Vietnam. The last man in the door was LT Bingham. I was at the bottom of the ladder, on our way in, with Macon right behind when we looked into Bingham's eyes as he closed the door on us. We banged on the locked door and yelled but got no response. We covered for each other and crossed the ground back to the tower. Once back at the tower we began to put out rounds. The tower was stocked with M-60, M-79, M-16 and LAWs. As we began to answer, the incoming withered at our end of the perimeter, the other end of the base was being overrun with only minimal return fire. We couldn't fire directly into that end of the base for fear of hitting our SVA allies. Macon did most of the firing while I brought in artillery and illumination from fire base Bastogne and Phu Bai. The attack had come from the west end of the base away from the river. Most of the attackers ran across the base towards the river where I attempted to bring artillery in on them. This wound up driving them back across the base to retreat back in the direction they had come from. By this time, we had gunships working over the ground outside the perimeter. Things had quieted down. The South Vietnamese went to work organizing their people and left us alone. Macon and I were pissed. We concluded that Bingham had locked us out, and the SVA weren't up to the fight. Macon must have said fifty times, "When Bingham comes out, I'm gonna kick his ass." After hearing this for several hours, I began to say it, too. "I'm gonna kick his ass." The morning hours were spent discussing all the ways and reasons we had for kicking Bingham's ass. By daylight we had ourselves convinced it was in his own best interest. When Bingham emerged from the French Maid at about eight in the morning, Macon and I kicked his ass. We then threw him on one of the birds hauling SVA to the hospital. It was our sincere hope that he would get the help that he needed there.

The next two days I was kept busy handling traffic for the teams and helping coordinate repairs to the perimeter. Seven SVA were killed in the attack, all newly minted medics. Macon and I were told that there would be disciplinary action over the incident involving LT Bingham. Macon told me that if I wanted, I could continue to work with MACV (Military Assistance Command, Vietnam), but I would have to make a decision very soon.

On the third morning after the attack Macon informed me that we were relocating to another base to the west. We had all of our gear ready for the move, and a helicopter picked us up at about ten in the morning. As soon as we had gained some altitude, Macon leaned over to me and asked if I wanted to stay with

MACV. I looked down and saw Fire Base Bastogne below and to the north of us. As we got closer to the border with Laos I said, "No, I don't want to continue with MACV." Macon spoke to one of the older guys. He spoke to the pilot, and we began our descent towards a little fire base west of Bastogne. It could have been Veghill. I'm not sure. I un-assed the bird and never saw any of those guys again.

I caught a ride on the next bird heading into the rear and made my way to the company area at Phu Bai. There I was called before our company commander and questioned about my involvement in the injuries sustained by LT Bingham a few days before. I was given the choice of accepting an article 15 or going before a court martial. I said I would accept the article 15, which is punishment doled out by the CO and doesn't go on record. I was given reduction in rank and one paygrade, and forfeiture of one week's pay for one month. My real punishment was being sent back out to hump the bush.

Back at the company area I rearmed myself and boarded a resupply helicopter out to the bush to rejoin my old platoon.

Since I had gone, LT Brown had returned to be the platoon leader. There was no love lost between us, and he proceeded to give me every shit job there was to remind me that he knew it was me that ratted him out to the CO on his previous screw ups. Add to that a bunch of new guys had come into the platoon in my absence, and I was out of shape from a month of hanging around the fort. We were in the lowlands to the northeast of Nui Que when we received word to move onto the mountain to once again act as a relay for other units operating in the area. From where we were at, it was an all-day hump to get into position. It was cloudy and humid and uphill the whole way. We reached the top of Nui-Que, just before nightfall in wind and rain. With a full platoon there was plenty of us to ring the hill with guard and fighting positions. LT Brown, personally, placed me in my guard position on solid rock overlooking the hill to the southwest. From where he had me set up, the wind blowing across the hill made it rain straight up, making seeing or hearing impossible. So, I moved back about ten feet where I could tuck in behind a boulder. From there the wind wasn't so strong, and every few seconds I could lean forward to see or hear and maintain my guard position. I hadn't been on watch for more than a half hour when the LT came to check on me. He gave me a raft of shit about not being in the proper guard position and had me move once again farther out on the rock. As soon as he went back to his shelter, I moved back to where I had been behind the rock. The rain slacked off, and the wind died down enough so that I could hear and see just a little. LT Brown had come out of his shelter and was sneaking up on me to try and catch me off guard. His hand touched my shoulder, and before he could say anything, I grabbed him by the front of his pants and threw him over the cliff. I could hear him land on the ledge about six or eight feet below my position. I let the bolt slam forward on my M-16 for emphasis and then called out, "Halt! Who goes there!"

"LT Brown, you shit head!" Came his answer. "Advance and be recognized!" I called. I could hear him scrambling around just below me. I gave him my hand to help him back up onto the top. We had a little discussion about the proper way to address someone on guard duty at night. He went back to his shelter as the rain and wind picked back up, and I heard no more from him that night.

By this time, I had been in country for over nine months. Most of the guys I'd come over with were being offered a two month drop. This would mean they could go back to the states after serving ten months in Vietnam. However, they would still have to serve out the rest of their enlistment stateside or at any post where the army wanted them. Most of the guys from the 101st were being sent to Fort Carson. Several of them sent letters informing us that returning draftees were being treated like crap. Guys who were leading squads in combat were being busted for minor infractions and then being told to pick up cigarette butts. This attitude was further fueled by the civilian and media bias against returning veterans. With my record of problems with authority, I figured I'd be better off in Nam than in the stateside army. If I returned to the states with less than five months remaining on my enlistment. I would process out of the army as soon as I got back to the states. With this in mind I soldiered on.

On the last day of our mission up on Nui Que, LT Brown came to me with a proposal. He would overlook my little indiscretion, if I would take on the role of squad leader and extend my tour of duty. In exchange I would get E-5 rank and be given a rear job to serve out my 13th and 14th months.

I instantly became an acting Buck Sergeant, squad leader. I never fooled myself that the Sergeant stripes would be forthcoming or that I'd get the cozy rear job. For crap sake, I was a draftee, 11-B, and the lowest form of army puke. I was proud to be serving my country and glad not to be a protester or a draft dodger. I would serve in Vietnam for another five months and get out when I got home with an honorable discharge. All I had to do was survive five more months.

SQUAD LEADER

We were pulled off Nui Que and brought back to Phu Bai for a couple of days. A bunch of new replacements came into the platoon filling the slots left by those who took their two month drops or were wounded or re-upped for a better job.

I now had a squad of all new guys except for me. The only other guy in the platoon that I knew from the beginning of my tour was John Fouts. He had become a squad leader when I was with

MACV. Although we were good friends, we seldom spoke on a personal level. By this time only a few of the old guys were still around. With all of the changing faces it becomes harder and harder to make attachments that experience tells you won't last.

By this time the 101st was the last full division in Vietnam. The war was being handed over to the South Vietnamese. We all knew how that was going. The new guys coming in were well aware of the situation. As other units pulled out, the 101 took on more and more operational responsibility. Smaller units were being sent to the field to cover more ground. The South Vietnamese could see the writing on the wall. There was more resentment between us and our allies. We still had to go to the field in search of a determined enemy. The overriding motivation became, "How do I survive this, and how do I keep my people from being injured or killed?"

My next trip to the bush would be with eleven new guys and myself. Don't get me wrong; these were good guys. Nearly all draftees like myself, mostly with the same eight weeks of basic training and nine weeks of infantry training. My most experienced guys were George Anderson and Jim Baker. They were six-month tour guys who had been in Germany for a year before being sent to Vietnam. By coincidence they had known each other in the states before being drafted. They had both been rodeo cowboys. George had ridden bucking horses, and Jim was a bull rider. They had come from the same area in Utah then came back together in my squad. There was a guy named Dean Keith from up around Astoria that sticks in my memory. There was a little black guy, kind of quiet who seemed to want to stay out of the way. I lost him on our first mission. I blocked him out of my memory for many years. He was new and obviously nervous.

We were being flown out to a ridge west of Bastogne. The LZ was on a side hill where the birds had to hover to drop us off, then do a half turn and depart the way they had come in. We would have to un-ass the birds at just the right second to hit the ground safely, then run to the sides to get clear of the spinning rotors, before the pilot swiveled the bird around to get out of there. When we loaded up, I put the little guy next to me on the right side of the bird. He sat to the front. Our legs dangled toward the skids as we approached the LZ. On approach it looked like we would fly right into the mountain. At the last second the pilot would flare and hover giving us a moment to hop to the ground. As we neared the LZ, I stepped down onto the skid and expected my man to do the same thing. As the mountain was coming up at us, I yelled, "Get ready to jump!" With the noise of Bird and background noise and the smoke from the recently lifted artillery barrage, I yelled again, "Get ready to jump!" I was expecting him to step down onto the skid in preparation for the insertion. At about twenty feet off the ground I yelled again, "Get ready to jump!"

He Jumped! From about fifteen feet with a full pack! I saw him crumple and go rolling down the hill below my feet. I got off the bird ran to the side and rolled out of my rucksack. I got to him where he came up against some brush in a little gully about sixty feet down the hill. His eyes were blank as I worked to untangle him from his rucksack and the brush. Both of his legs were broken just above his boot tops, and he was completely limp. John Fouts appeared next to me just then, and the two of us drug him back up the hill by his arms. There were still birds coming in, and we managed to get him onto the next one by hoisting him up to our shoulders and tossing him in. He never said a word the whole time. Just gazed straight ahead. I sometimes wonder what happened to him. A brave little guy who answered the call and never got a chance to fire his weapon. Now I wonder what he was thinking as he tumbled down that hill in enemy territory with two broken legs. His jungle fatigues and boots were covered with blood and the bone protruded from both legs.

The last of the birds came in. We secured the area and made preparation to move out. As I said, I blocked this from my memory for many years. Perhaps because of guilt that I was his squad leader and didn't protect him or prepare him as good as I could have. Maybe it was just a small footnote in a war where a lot of things didn't make sense.

Our platoon moved away from the LZ up the ridge. We spent the rest of that day moving along the ridge probing into areas where we suspected enemy activity. In the afternoon we moved off the ridge into thick vegetation.

I had ten new guys to bring up to speed, to school them in how to deploy a claymore mine so as to defend our night position or to be effective in an ambush. Over and over I asked myself these questions. Who has the right stuff to walk point? Do I have the best guy on the gun? Is my RTO keeping the communications open and his radio working?

I had Baker on point and Anderson walking slack as we pushed off the ridge down into triple canopy. Several times I called a halt and made my way up to the point to bring the squad's attention to signs that the enemy had passed through here not long before us. I was pointing out tracks on the trail and discussing with the point how old they might be. I had to keep reminding myself that these guys were brand new to the bush. At the same time, I was fighting back the urge to call them a bunch of newbie pukes that were intent on getting us all killed. I found a place to get them all off the trail, and we formed up a little perimeter with everyone within a couple of feet of one another. They could all hear me as I talked in a whisper. I addressed them as miserable puke bastards that were going to be dead if they didn't get their shit together. Quit bitching and work as a team. Our job for today was to scout this trail. None of us wants to be on a trail being used by the enemy, so let's gather the information and get out of here in good health. When we moved out, everyone was a little quieter and taking the job more seriously. I was walking third man in support of the point team where I could keep eyes on the trail myself. Another trail merged with the first one and the signs of traffic grew heavier. We had been on the larger trail for maybe 200 feet when I raised my arm to stop the squad. I gave them a sign to take up a defensive position and signaled the point man to come to me. When he reached me, he could tell I was furious with him. I could see that he didn't have a clue why I had stopped him. I reached off to the right of the trail and pointed out two human hairs tangled on a bush. I moved the branches aside and Indicated on the ground where someone had squatted to pee. I pulled Baker to me and whispered in his ear, "You see these long black hairs Baker? Who do you think they belong to Baker? Smell that pee Baker? How big a unit do you think passed by here Baker? Don't you think we all deserve to know about this kind of shit? Open your eyes! It is your job to see this shit first. It's not likely that a woman was out here alone. There is a bunch of gooks here somewhere, and we don't want to meet them on their terms." I pointed out the hair to each man and had them smell the pee. Everything counts in the bush. When we continued on, the pucker factor was way up.

Judging by the signs, there had to be a company down there at least. If we could find their location, we could pull back and call in an air strike on them. The trick would be to remain undetected long enough to accomplish that. We found a place where we could set up above the trail about fifty meters. We had a good escape route up the hill to our back in the direction we would have to go to rejoin the rest of the platoon. We had been on the move for more than four hours, and we needed a break. I set up two guys where they could watch the trail, and the rest of us hunkered down to eat some C-rations and drink some water laced with halazone.

Baker signaled me to come look. I moved up next to him and observed movement below us on the trail. Thirty-four NVA passed by, all carrying weapons and loaded down with equipment. There were no women with them. I got on the radio to call it in, but we were out of communication. We saddled up and began to move back up the hill in the direction of our platoon.

Baker and Anderson were at point, and the pucker factor was through the roof. I didn't hear a piece of equipment or a single sound as we climbed up out of that canyon. Near the crest of the hill we were able to reestablish communications. I called in our position and reported what we had seen. Our orders were to join the rest of the platoon to establish an NDP site. An hour later we moved inside the relative safety of the platoon perimeter.

I reported to the LT along with the other three squad leaders. Two of the other squads had seen evidence of troop movements, but ours was the only squad to have actually seen troops on the move. The canyon where we had observed the troops was out of reach from any of our artillery. An ARA observer flew out and buzzed up and down the canyon but could not see anything from the air. The canopy was just too thick down there.

We had a couple of hours to rest until we moved into our NDP. I set up the guys in three-man positions and leaned back on my ruck to take a snooze. The Ukrainian and Bro were pulling watch about six feet from me as I laid there with my eyes closed listening to their whispered voices. I kept hearing them refer to Gook Man this and Gook Man that. I realized they were talking about me. Bro couldn't believe I had seen those hairs along the trail, and then had everyone smell the pee. The Ukrainian said, "Man, I'm glad he got us out of there before that bunch of NVA came down the trail." I remember thinking, "Man, were we lucky, and God had been good to us again."

December 1970. Bravo company had been in the field for several weeks. We were in the highlands west of Hue. It had been raining the entire mission while we stalked an elusive enemy through thick triple canopy. Word came down that we would be extracted to the rear to dry out for a couple of days, if we could get down out of the jungle where the helicopters could lift us out. Over a hundred of us slogged down the mountains heading for our extraction point. Our platoon was on point as we slipped and slid down the trail, each man keeping in sight of the guy in front of him. Every few minutes someone would go careening out of control often taking out the guy in front of him as we slithered our way forward.

On our second day of movement John's squad was on point and my squad right behind. We were at a place where the jungle was giving way to more open places at the tops of the ridgelines. We took a break at about noon to eat some C's when we saw some hats moving up the ridge line towards us. The conical head gear of four Vietnamese bobbed along above the grass perhaps a half mile down slope from us. About the time we finished our break the four Vietnamese kids reached the point man. The company commander and his interpreter had made their way to the front of the column to greet them and find out what was going on. It turned out they were from a village that we would pass through most likely the next day, and they had come out to sell us sodas and sandwiches. I bought a cold coke and a sandwich before they could be bought out. It was a rare treat to get anything but C's in the field.

While the company commander was at the head of the column, he received a message from the TOC that we wouldn't be brought out to the rear but instead would be transported from our pickup point to Fire support base Rakkasan to reinforce another company that was there and being probed by a large force of NVA that were building up around the fire base. When the news spread through the company, every one's attitude went to shit. As we got closer to the low lands, our chances of getting birds increased, but so did our chances of hitting booby traps or contact. We were instructed to loiter in the area for the day and make our way to our extraction point the next day.

Next day my squad was on point for the company. About nine in the morning we spotted the conical hats coming up the ridgeline towards us once again. Again, they sold cokes and sandwiches and went on their way. I saw them disappear down the ridge and reappear on the other side of a little knoll. They had changed their route from the day before choosing to go around the knoll on the opposite side. As we moved closer to the area, I became more and more paranoid. I took over the point position as we neared the knoll. I had slowed the company movement to a crawl then stopped it all together when I spotted an unexploded 105 round about five feet off the trail. It was not uncommon to find dud rounds, but this one did not look right to me. I got on the radio and called back to the CO to let him know what was going on. He said he would send up his artillery observer to have a look. In minutes the LT arty guy was telling me to put a pound of C-4 next to it and blow it in place. I instructed two of my guys to get the longest piece of bamboo they could find. We fastened a bar of C-4 to the end of it inserting an electric blasting cap hooked to a claymore wire. Several times the CO and the arty LT were back on the radio wanting to know what the holdup was. I wasn't satisfied until we had three claymore wires hooked together end to end and were below the crest of the ridge behind a stump. The LT was back up front again telling me, "It's just a 105 round. Blow it and let's get out of here." I wanted to tell him to fuck off, but somehow managed to squash that comment and keep to the task at hand. Jim, George and I were huddled down behind the stump when I yelled, "Fire in the hole!" and depressed the handle of the claymore clicker. There was a huge explosion. Dirt and debris went skyward for several seconds. A piece of stump that must have weighed 600 pounds careened over our heads and landed down slope. Lighter materials, sticks and dirt made a hissing noise as they fell back to earth through the trees. Everyone in the company felt the dirt raining down. No one was hurt. We rolled up our claymore wire and continued to march. Neither the CO nor the LT had anything to say as the company moved past that thirty-foot hole in the ground. It was only ten in the morning.

We circled around the village in order to make it to our pick-up point on time. We moved onto and secured the LZ which was clear enough to receive our incoming birds. My squad was on the first bird out. Just after we lifted off Dean pulled a bottle of Jack

Daniels out of his ruck and passed it around. It helped to cut the

chill in that open helicopter flying through the fog looking for a

way into Rakkasan. The bottle passed from grunt to grunt then to

the two door gunners then to the pilot and co-pilot. When it

reached Dean again, there was about a half a sip left. He

knocked it down as we all looked on. With a look of despair on

his face he flung the empty into the fog. The pilot turned his head

with a big smile on his face as he extracted another bottle of Jack

from beneath his seat. One turn around the Huey and that bottle,

too, joined its brother on its earthward trip.

   Rakkasan was socked in. So, we would be dropped at the

bottom of the hill in the lowlands and have to hump our way onto

the hill. We formed up at our drop off point and began to move up

the road that served as a supply road onto the fire base when dry

weather allowed. We moved up the road in a column of twos with

John Fouts at the head of the left column and me at the head of

the right. We had over a hundred men behind us and an open

line to the artillery at the top of the hill we were climbing up.

Several times we halted the company while we called in mortars

to deal with small arms fire that came at us from the sides of the road. By humping all day, we came onto the fire base a little before dusk.

We had been able to smell hot chow for the past several hours. Our noses led us straight to a mess tent. As we were about to enter, a big old mess sergeant blocked our entry saying that we were infantry and that this was an artillery mess tent. John and I had already encroached far enough to see the steam tables full of the stuff we had been smelling for the past hours as we climbed through the muck to come and reinforce these SOB's. I started to explain our point of view to the mess sergeant and thought that I might succeed in getting him to bend the rules when John rendered my argument moot by tossing a fragmentation grenade into the mess sergeant's kitchen. As the mess crew ducked for cover, the mess was overwhelmed by hungry grunts filling anything they could get their hands on with hot chow and coffee. By the time the CO and the rest of the company filed onto the hill, the grenade incident was just some rumor started by a disgruntled mess sergeant.

John and I had just led the company onto FSB- Rakkasan. We were two of the oldest guys in the company with nearly twelve months in country, and it was just about Christmas. My squad was assigned a bunker looking to the north. We searched out our fields of fire, secured our positions and settled in for the night. The bunkers on Rakkasan were by no means comfortable but they offered a lot more than the jungle during monsoon season.

Listening out into the night through the mist we could hear truck motors and equipment being moved around. It seemed impossible that the NVA could have that kind of resources in that terrain, but that is what we were hearing. I took the last guard from three in the morning till sun up. Just as the sun began to light the area through the fog, I glanced over and saw Tiny, a big guy from one of the other platoons. He was standing up on the sand bags pissing down the hill. Now these sand bags were woven out of plastic fabric, so they were slippery with the dew on them. I was thinking it was a little dumb to be exposing one's self to sniper fire so early in the day. I studied the terrain in front of my position as dawn continued to change the seen below me. I heard Tiny cry out for help and saw him hovering above the ground below his bunker. He was wailing and half screaming as I made my way to him. He had slipped off the sand bag wall that made up the front of his bunker. From there he had fallen about six feet to where he became impaled on an engineer's stake up his ass. The top of the stake was about six feet off the ground and mushroomed over from having been driven in with a sledge hammer. All I could do was to lift him to ease some of the weight that held him to the stake and yell for assistance. Within minutes there were four of us working to free him from the stake, but the hill was so steep and the sandbag wall so slippery that we couldn't get much traction to push him upward and off the stake. With four guys above with ropes pulling up and four of us below pushing we were able to tear him free from his impalement. He never lost consciousness as we got him onto a stretcher and up to the aid station. That morning as we went to chow, there was Tiny kneeling over the end of a cot with an IV in one end and a drain in the other. He was pretty well sedated as we gave him a hard time about what great lengths some guys would go to get out of Nam.

Rakkasan was socked in, no birds in or out for days. Tiny languished at the door of the aid station, and the platoons stared down the hill into the fog listening. About our fourth night on the hill, a newly minted LT came around asking if anyone would like to go with him on a night operation outside the wire. He quizzed the whole company and as far as I know got no takers. It was

New Year's Day 1971, and moral was at an all-time low. I hadn't spoken to John since the grenade went off in the mess tent. I just wanted to endure until my tour was over. I believe it was on the second of January the fog cleared off, and resupply could get in. I remember a shiny looking Huey made it in and I thought, "Oh great! The brass is coming out to give us shit about something." Turned out it was the first sergeant come out to the field to make sure we got paid. I didn't bother going over to get my mail or to collect my pay.

One of my guys, George Anderson, came to me and said he got a rear job. "A rear job!" I said. "Who gave it to you?" "The first shirt. He is up at the TOC, with pay and mail." I immediately proceeded in the direction of the TOC to get the straight up from the first shirt. "What is this I hear about you giving Anderson a rear job? Why would Anderson get a rear job?" "Oh, he and Baker have the most time, in country." "No, he does not, Top. I have the most time in country and so does John Fouts. He and I came to the unit on the same day." "Well, who are you?" "I'm Diaper Dan!" "Nope!" he says, "Diaper Dan left two months ago." "I'm telling you, I'm Diaper Dan." Several guys standing nearby confirmed saying, "He's Diaper Dan alright." The top said, "Ok!

Get those travel orders back from Anderson and Baker, and I'll reissue them to you and Fouts." I made my way back to the bunker line and got the travel orders back from Anderson and Baker. The disappointment on their faces was unmistakable, as I told Anderson that he would be taking over as squad leader and gave him my map case and wished him good luck. Instead of getting a rear job, he got the worst job… my job. I said a quick goodbye to the rest of my squad and proceeded to hunt down John.

I found him in his bunker in a surly mood. I stood outside in some of the first sunshine we had seen in weeks while he sat back in the dark bunker unseen. I said, "John, we got rear jobs." At first, he didn't answer at all. I said John, "We got fucking rear jobs." He said, "Don't fuck with me, man." I waved the travel papers where he could see them and said John, "We got real fucking rear jobs and real fucking travel papers." He said, "Don't fuck with me, man." But now he came forward enough that I could see his face in the light. I shook the travel vouchers before him and lured him out of the bunker. We walked together up to the TOC where he spoke to the Top and became convinced that it was real.

The Top told us to wait on the chopper pad for the first bird headed for the rear. John and I made our way down to the pad and found a spot to sit and light up a smoke. Just after we lit up, a Huey came in. It was all spit shined and looking like an officer's bird, so we didn't pay it any mind. A few seconds later I looked down to see a pair of spit shined boots standing in front of me. John and I both looked up into the eyes of no less than General Westmoreland. We sprang to our feet putting out our smoke and snapping what I hoped was an acceptable salute. The general asked what we were doing, and I replied that we were in transit to the rear after serving twelve months in the bush. He thanked us for our service and wished us good fortune for the remainder of our tour. A few minutes later a rough-looking Huey bumped down and kicked off a load of freight. We boarded that bird and were in bound for Phu Bai and our company area.

THE REAR

Upon entering the company area, we found that there was a new rule in effect that our weapons had to be locked up while we were in the rear. It felt unnatural after carrying an M-16 for so long to be without it. We checked in with the company clerk and headed for the showers. After the showers John needed to go to the dentist for a tooth that was paining him. I went back to the clerk to ask where Mike Corral was. Mike had come over the same day as John and I and was one of the few old timers left around. He was also my best friend. The company clerk told me that Mike was in the hospital and that he was being transported to a hospital ship. If I wanted to see him, I would have to make haste. I left immediately and was able to catch a ride in the direction of the EVAC hospital in Phu Bai.

A nurse guided me through a maze of wards and tents to the one that held Mike. He had tubes in his nose and arm and was not aware of my presence. As I stood there looking at my best friend, she said that she was just about to administer a shot that would bring him around in order that he could be transported to a hospital ship. I had come at just the right time to be there when he woke up. As Mike began to come around, the nurse left us alone for a few minutes.

When Mike could recognize that it was me standing next to his bed, a smile cracked around the tubes and wires coming from his face. I told him they were going to transport him to a hospital ship in a few minutes and that he had the million-dollar wound. "Where is your Purple Heart? How did this happen in the rear?"

Mike was a jeep driver for a full-bird colonel since he came out of the field several weeks ago. I figured they had been fired on somewhere off base, and Mike had been hit. I was wrong. Mike told me what happened. They had taken out his dentures, so he wouldn't choke on them with the tubes and the pain medications. With his Spanish accent it was likely that I was the only person at that time who could understand him. As he labored through the telling of it, I was able to get a picture of what had unfolded leading up to his injuries.

Things began to go wrong when the company clerk assigned Mike to a hooch with six black guys who had recently been transferred into our company. These guys had been passed around from unit to unit when they refused to go to the field and had problems with drug usage and trafficking. They refused to fight the white man's war. On the night before I came out of the field, Mike was told to go in and wake up one of the guys for guard duty out on the base perimeter. The guy, angered by

Mike's insistence that he get up for guard duty, rose up with a combat knife and stabbed Mike seven times.

Right after telling me his story, Mike was loaded onto a helicopter and was on his way out to the hospital ship. I made my way back to the company area. My high at getting out of the field was blown. After twelve months humping the bush Mike had been brought low by a pissed off malcontent over getting up for guard duty.

I walked in on the company clerk and sat on the edge of his desk while he gave me his version of how things had gone down. I asked him who these guys were and which hooch they were in. His rendition of the events meshed with Mike's pretty well, except that he failed to elaborate on what in God's name he was thinking when he billeted a patriotic Mexican-American in with six malcontent, antiwar black guys.

The clerk got up and went into an adjoining room to answer a phone. He had left a drawer open at the right of his desk, where I could see a forty-five and two loaded magazines. I picked up the 1911 with my right hand inserting one of the magazines into the butt of the gun and worked the slide to lock and load. I placed the second magazine in the left pocket of my jungle fatigues, next to one of the two grenades I had held back when we locked up our weapons. Exiting the company clerk's office, I made my way towards the hooch where Mike had been stabbed. Nearing the location, I could hear music turned up a little loud for late afternoon. It was Tina Turner belting out something about being done wrong. As she wailed, I pulled the pin on the grenade and breathed in the smell of dope and incense that permeated from the hooch. I held the grenade high in my left hand with my thumb on the spoon. The forty-five was in my right hand at eye level as I entered. The occupants of the hooch backed away from me towards the back of the room. The biggest one of them was the one I suspected of working Mike over. He laid on his cot coming to a sitting position as a string of obscenities left my mouth. I could see terror in the eyes of all six of them. The music screamed, and a tape played in my head, "You pull this trigger and you will never go home. You pull this trigger, and you will never go home." I wanted one of them to make a move, so that I could start the killing. None of them moved, I backed out of their hooch with the music still blaring and my string of foul oaths hanging in the air.

Outside I felt like a coward for not having killed the bunch of them. Up until today I had spent the last twelve months trying to kill NVA. Yet, faced with these cowards I could not pull the trigger knowing it would keep me from ever going home.

I needed time to think. I went to my hooch to try and bring myself together. It was beginning to get dark when I finished making up a dummy in my cot to fool the Black Panthers. I placed a claymore on the ground beneath the floor aiming it to take out whoever might come after me. I ran the claymore wire over to under the next hooch where I laid all night waiting for them to come for me.

Before dawn John came looking for me. He crawled under the hooch with me and told me that the six black guys had been suddenly transferred out to another unit in the middle of the night after complaining to the CO about some crazy-off-his-rocker grunt threatening to kill them all. He said that they wanted us out of the company area and that we were being transported to Tan My by truck right after chow.

The company clerk gave us our travel orders, and we got our weapons back to travel to Tan My. Our route would take us up highway one through Hue City then east toward the coast. We boarded a sampan on the beach that ferried us the two miles or so out to the island and landed us at the village at the north end of the island. From there John and I walked with our gear to Eagle Beach stand down area and reported in to the unit commander. He was a captain with just a couple of weeks left in country. We saluted him, and he handed us over to his first sergeant to get us settled and show us around. We were now part of the cadre which amounted to about a platoon of us. Our duties consisted of maintaining the guard positions between us and a village that occupied the south end of the island and manning a thirty-foot-high guard tower that commanded a three-hundred-and-sixty-degree view of the area. I was assigned as sergeant of the guard of the west bunker that faced the village and the view across the water back towards Hue City. My job would be to maintain a constant presence at the bunker twenty-four hours a day to monitor traffic on and off the base from the village or from the water to the west. Every morning people from the village would come to the gate on their way to jobs on the base where they cleaned or cut hair or worked at the EM club. On an average day five to ten people would pass through the gate in the morning then back through when their work was done. Others would pass through to catch the boat to the main land or visit relatives in the village at the north end of the island. One person who came through the gate every day was the whore who worked in the village. She would pass through to go get checked out by the medics at our aid station. If she was found to have any disease, that information would be passed on to us, and we would attempt to keep the GI's from visiting her. This would turn out to be one of the hardest things to do.

Night after night drunk and stoned GI's would come to the gate to pass through to go see Babe-Son for some boom-boom. In the past it had been learned that not all of them would be persuaded by telling them that the village was off limits or that the whore had the clap when tested that day. They could walk in the water out around the ends of our bunker lines with nothing to stop them but a bullet from one of us. We weren't going to do that. So, the policy that developed was to talk them out of it, if possible, and if not, to hold their valuables and extra cash until they returned. The Babe–Son and the Mama-Son had many relatives that lived in the village. Some of whom were South Vietnamese soldiers. It wasn't uncommon for a group of them to relieve a GI of his watch or money and dump them unconscious on the beach to find their way back to the base when they came to. Most nights a group of two to five or six guys would come to the gate and demand that we let them through. I would talk to them and tell them of the conditions in the village and try to dissuade them. They would call me a REMF and say that I didn't know what is was like to be out in the bush. I would reply that all of us here were infantry who had spent most of our tours in the bush and had the honor of serving out our last few weeks here on Tan-My. After hearing my little speech, most of the guys would head back to the base and the enlisted men's club. For those few that refused, we held their valuables, if they would let us, until they returned.

About three weeks into my time at Tan-My we got a new Commanding Officer, he was an Airborne Ranger, Panama Jungle School, newly minted Lieutenant. He seemed like a nice enough guy, but way too full of gung ho. I have no idea how he got a slot out here with all of us short timers when he was new to the war. One night he came out to the bunker line to check things out for himself. He had checked out the bunker on the opposite side of the road and was inspecting our position when a group of GI's showed up to go out the gate. It must have been around nine or ten at night. I gave them my usual speech including news that the one whore in the village had the clap as reported by the medics today. Most of the guys believed me and even in their less than sober state were willing to return to the base. Two of the group were not to be turned aside and insisted that if we did not open the gate, they would walk around. The LT pointed his weapon at them and warned them to turn around. When neither of them did, he fired into the ground near their feet. The one nearest to us came back, but the other guy kept on walking with the LT firing rounds near his feet the whole way. Thank God none of those guys had weapons. Judging by the words coming out of their mouths and the looks in their eyes the LT wouldn't have lived through the next couple of seconds. The lone GI blended into the darkness in the direction of the village. In the meantime, the rest of the group were expressing their displeasure with the LT to the point where he brandished his weapon at them. Everyone could see how pumped up and fearful he was and that made them hate him even more. Several of my guys moved forward out of the darkness near the bunker. Nobody raised a weapon. It was merely to let everyone know they were there. Things became calm at that moment. I wished the group well on the remainder of their time at Eagle Beach and safety for the rest of their tour. The LT was still burning with adrenaline after firing his weapon and being humiliated by the group of grunts. After the group was gone for a few minutes, the LT got it together enough to make his way back to the company area and the safety of his office.

John and I and Insane and the rest of the guys at the bunker talked through the night about how screwed up the LT was and how lucky he was that no more went wrong than did. Someone could have easily been killed. Nobody wanted it to be them.

The lone GI who went to the village showed up at the gate around four in the morning looking like he'd been drug through a knothole backward. He spent enough time with us to smoke a cigarette then headed off toward the base with a big smile on his face.

A Philippine band played at the EM club twice a day for the GI's on stand down. None of them spoke English good enough to carry on a conversation, but the female lead singer knew a few words. She fronted for the band and spoke a little between songs. The band had learned the lyrics to American music by memorizing the sounds of the words and were able to pump out a recognizable version of maybe fifty songs. Louie-Louie and Danny Boy were included in every set.

We had a guy named Leonard with us, a big ole boy from the Midwest. He went by Lenny and was madly in love with the little Philippine lead singer. She would come out and set with us during breaks. She and Lenny would gush over each other. Poor Lenny was head over heels for her. He would get mad at us if we didn't applaud after each one of her songs. Lenny would say, "That was a beautiful rendition of 'Wake up little Susie'." Only it sounded like, "Wait hup a lis uzzie wait hup." We would laugh and laugh, and Lenny would get mad as hell at us. He took to sitting alone with her to protect her from our rude behavior. They made an odd couple, but it was the closest thing to love any of us had seen for a while.

We were all broken and hungry for something that war couldn't touch. Even here at Eagle Beach, we found that the war could still get to us. An incident took place that would once again change my perspective on the war when a case of fragmentation grenades came up missing from the bunker across the road from mine. The sergeant in charge at the time was questioned by the LT as to what might have happened to them. He said he thought the kids from the village took them while the guys were kept occupied playing soccer with a group of them. From the beginning I thought this was Bogus! The Sergeant making the accusation had three days left to go in country, so the last thing he wanted was to do anything that might delay his departure. What I think is that the Navy guys from the Riverine Patrol at the other end of the island needed the ordinance and traded for them with the sergeant or got him drunk or stoned and stole them. The Navy there seemed to have a hard time keeping small arms ordinance on hand for their trips up the river. We often gave them M-16, M-60 and 45 ammo from our stores, so that they could make their runs up the river fully armed. As with any trade between the army and the navy, the deal was all the sweeter if you could just steal it. Anyway, the frags were missing and the sergeant was processing out to head home, when the LT announced that we are going to sweep the village in search of the missing grenades. John and I both tried to talk the LT out of the sweep, but he was determined to find those grenades along with any other contraband that might be in the village that had been taken from the base.

At 7:00 AM we began our sweep with most of a platoon. John and about two squad's worth of us had the southwest end of the sweep along the beach and to the center of the island. The village was laid out with houses facing each other across a small sand street. The back yards were garden areas often with some trees and palms and a ditch for sewage. I took up a position to the far right in the direction of march along the beach that faced the mainland. While we were still in the garden area of the first row of houses, one of the guys at the other end of the line found what he thought was some stolen property. We converged on that point as the LT came up to have a look. Two women and an old Papa-San were spread eagle on the ground when we walked up. The LT had his weapon on them along with several other guys. The younger woman I recognized as a maid who came onto the base most days to clean. She cried and screamed and got all defiant to the LT saying, "Me no Cowboy, Me no cowboy. I'm no thief, I'm no thief." She spit at the LT and called him, "Number ****** ten thou GI." One of the guys spoke up and said that the radio had belonged to one of his hooch mates that had gone home a few days before. He said the gook girl stole it.

Some South Vietnamese troops became present about then, and it was plain to see they didn't like what was developing.

The pucker factor jumped up by a factor of ten as we got back on line to search the next row of houses. Now we had all of the villagers aroused from the maid to the village head man. As we began to move forward again, I crossed over the beach to check out two small sampans that were pulled up just at the water's edge. They were both empty save for the paddles that belonged with them. I crossed back to the second row of houses and took up a position at the corner of the first structure I came to. It turned out to be a parsonage where the local Buddhist Priest lived. From that spot I could look into the backyards of several houses to the east into their garden areas. Nestled into what looked like green beans growing up a trellis I saw two young boys in black pajamas. Concealed in some bushes at the corner of the house, I watched them through the sights of my M-16. As I watched they began to move in the direction of the sampans. When they stepped away from the trellis, I could see they had no weapons and weren't carrying anything at all. They looked to me like they were just trying to get the hell out of there. As they crossed into the open headed for the sampans, the LT spotted them. They had just enough time to push off from shore when they were consumed in a hail of small arms fire. The LT and several others waded out into the knee-deep water to bring their trophies back to shore.

I did not want to fire on those boys in the sampan, but I did. Once you start in on killing someone you want to get it done all the way. When their boats met the shore, I saw their blood stain the water and the sand as it leaked out through the new bullet holes. When I heard the LT say something about a body count into the radio, anger flooded into me. I was supposed to be done with this. To hear this LT crowing into the radio, I was pissed. As the sweep continued, I went back to my position by the parsonage. In the front of the parsonage there was a coconut palm with a few nuts hanging from it. I found myself firing my weapon into those coconuts. I must have fired about three clips when a Buddhist Monk stepped into my field of vision. He was dressed in an intricately embroidered blue silk robe with a tiny hat that matched and had a little scrawny beard in two braids. I pointed my weapon at his chest as he approached to within three feet of me. He began to speak, "Ding Dow Bick None Sing Dat." Hell, I didn't have a clue what he was saying. But the little guy looked me straight in the eye and kept talking like he was selling me a new Buick. He took another step forward, talking the whole time, and put his hand on the barrel of my M-16 brushing it aside. Inside of my head I'm screaming, "Shoot the SOB!" but another voice was saying, "You are going to see this guy in heaven."

I had reached the end. I knew that I could no longer continue. I made some kind of apology to the old monk and walked back to base. The rest of the platoon finished the sweep and returned to base about a half hour after me.

John told me that the rest of the mission netted nothing, and the only contraband item was the radio and a few other things. No proof that anyone had stolen anything. So, we had an hour or so under the leadership of the LT destroy any good will between us and the village.

It ain't nothing but a thing. Just another day in the Nam. Two more weeks to go. Those last two weeks crawled by at a snail's pace, pulling guard duty and avoiding contact with the LT as much as I could. On my last day at Tan-My, John and I rose early and gathered our gear for the trip back to the company area at Phu-Bai. We caught the boat to the mainland; then hitched a ride on a fuel truck headed for Phu-Bai. The drivers were always happy to have a little more security with them.

When we got back to base, we began processing out. I handed my M-16 into the Armorer, he checked the serial number and signed my paperwork.

John and I spent the last night in the company area drinking beer at the EM club. At some point during the evening, I stepped outside to smoke a joint and get some fresh air. In the distance, out to the west, tracers were pouring down from a gunship. More tracers crisscrossed not far from the first ones, and I could hear the distant impact of artillery. Part of me longed to be out there… Part of me realized, I would never again feel the rush of survival that comes after a firefight or know the creeping secretive fear of observing the enemy at close quarters when he does not know you are there. To know the hot burning rush of sitting in the door of a Huey and the ground rushing up as we drop into a hot LZ. To look around and see the faces of the pilot and door gunners and my fellow grunts as we fire our weapons into the rushing terrain. Jumping off into the unknown into whatever today's piece of jungle has to offer. No more would I sweat under the crushing load of a rucksack full of munitions for the chance to play tag with the enemy. All of the survival skills that I had so tirelessly honed would slip away if not continually kept polished.

After a while of staring into the night, I rejoined John and the others in the EM club. Clyde the Sniper had joined our table and greeted me with a cold beer. Clyde was in the rear for a three day in country R and R and was heading back out to his unit the next day. It was the end of February 1971. Clyde said he had been down to Dan Nang and spent a couple of days at a beach near there populated mostly by Air force guys. He said the racial tensions were worse there than here, especially at night with soldiers having to travel in groups in order to keep from being beat up. John and I laughed at that. Hell, we got "Dear John" letters months ago. From the news, we hear that the chicks back home want nothing to do with returning Vets, and now we are wrong for being white, too. Sounds like a whole lot of shit we can't do nothing about. Clyde wished us well on our last days in the Army and cautioned us to take it easy on the REMF's we would meet while processing out.

May first, John and I traveled to Dan Nang and then Can Ron Bay to continue processing out. I think it was here that I had to present myself to the Enlistment Officer. Before I walked in, I had convinced myself that I was going to re-up. I was going to cut the best deal I could for myself, use the reenlistment bonus to buy a car, then spend a month traveling before coming back to Nam for another tour. When I was called into the enlistment office, I couldn't believe my eyes. The sergeant I would reenlist with was a guy I knew from high school. He was a couple of years ahead of me in school and always a bully. He liked to push around anyone smaller than him. He recognized me instantly and acted like we were old pals. During our conversation I made it clear that I would not be reenlisting, so he asked me to speak to another recruiter. I was passed down the hall to a man who worked for the government of Laos. He informed me that my skills were needed in his country and that I would be paid well and have regular time out of the field should I accept his offer to come to work for him. At that time my Army pay amounted to about three hundred fifty dollars per month. Laos was offering me over two thousand a month to do the same thing. Part of me was saying, "Hell, Yes," but the other part was saying, "God has preserved me through some pretty rough spots. This wouldn't be for God and country." This was something different. It sounded good, two weeks in the field then two weeks in Thailand. I'd need to sign a one-year contract.

All those nights of praying to God that he would let me make it home again? Here I was placing it all on the scales for a chance to make what to me was some serious money. I turned it down. I went outside and found a circle of guys smoking pot and joined in. Our freedom bird was offloading the new meat, and we would be boarding to leave in short order.

Aboard the plane it was stifling hot setting there on the runway. Guys were flirting with the flight attendants and trying to distract themselves from the fear that at the last minute a rocket or a mortar was going to change everything. Sitting there stuffed into that aluminum tube I was trying to put a brave face on my claustrophobia. Minutes passed like hours before we slowly began to roll down the runway. Everyone remained restrained while the plane climbed, and the air conditioning began to catch up. Somewhere a few minutes out the pilot announced that we were out of Vietnam's air space. Joy and laughter broke out from one end of the plane to the other, and the flight attendants served drinks to all that wanted them. We stopped for fuel in Japan then flew the polar route to Anchorage then down to

McCord. The Army had a bus there that hopped us over to Fort Lewis for processing. All of us who were leaving the Army were separated out right after our steak dinner. Some non-com lined us up in a parking lot and tried to make us pick up cigarette butts. Several of us told him to go fuck himself, and he warned us that he could delay our separation from the military should he choose to do so. We reminded him that we could permanently delay his walk across this parking lot if he wanted to press the issue. He opted to focus his harassment on some easier pickings.

Several hours later I was at a small bus stop on I-5 at Fort Lewis waiting for a bus that would take me down to Salem, Oregon. While setting there in my dress greens, I was thinking of the past fourteen months. It was the first time I'd worn the dress uniform since just before I left for Nam. I was proud to have served and was reflecting on having survived my tour. Two guys and a girl entered the small bus stop and walked towards where I was sitting. I thought, "Cool, someone to talk to." As they came within talking distance, I heard them call me a baby killer. One of the guys spat at me. I could feel my M-16 in my hands. I could feel the bolt slam forward as I clicked off the safety and turned loose a burst in their direction. The room spun around a couple of times, and I came to my feet as they made for the exit.

My God, what just happened? My bus pulled up outside. As I climbed aboard, I noticed a look of distain in the eyes of some of my fellow passengers. No one spoke to me the entire trip. My bus arrived in Salem at around five in the afternoon on a Saturday. Dad was there to pick me up in the old green VW bug. His first words to me were "I'll bet you'll be glad to get out of that uniform."

Over forty years have passed since my return from Vietnam. Here are my final thoughts. The country I was sent to war to preserve no longer exists. Its flag is just a memory for old people. It doesn't appear that our leaders have learned a great deal from our ten years there. We are still getting involved in conflicts that seem to have no resolution. Our blood, which is our greatest treasure, is still flowing from our bodies onto the sand in other countries. What makes us do it? For me it is an idea… the Idea that we can choose our leaders in a nonviolent way. Our yearning to offer freedom to others and to foster and protect those freedoms. This ideal is something I still believe and the reason I feel it is time to tell my story, a story of a young man who served in Vietnam, who didn't run away from his country's call and weathered the storms of war as best as any 19-year-old kid could do. This is the story of Diaper Dan.

PARTING SHOTS

Janet and I have four children and ten grandchildren. It is an honor and privilege to see them all making their way through life in this wonderful country. They all have definite ideas about who should be in charge and how their tax dollars are spent. Power to the people, women's liberation, equal rights, gay rights, abortion rights, gender discrimination, immigration rights, animal rights, border control and the list grows daily.

Within our system all these issues can be reconciled. Out of all of my experiences, I have learned one thing above all others. We live in a great country. The basic tenets laid down in our constitution and bill of rights make room for clarity and solution when we as a people work together. God Bless America!

349

355

Made in the USA
San Bernardino, CA
18 February 2020